Jewels of the Romanovs

STEFANO PAPI

Jewels of the Romanovs
FAMILY & COURT

ON PAGE 1: A diamond and peridot bow brooch of the mid-18th century, in the collection of the Russian State.

ON PAGES 2–3: A jewel that appeared in a sale at Sotheby's in Geneva on 17 November 2005, which combines two the Russian State jewels sold at Christie's in London on 16 March 1927: a diamond necklace of the second half of the 18th century from the Imperial Treasury (lot 71) and a diamond knot of ribband ornament of the mid-18th century (lot 42). They were joined together after the 1927 sale.

Numbers in square brackets, e.g. [225], indicate the page on which an illustration appears.

© 2010 Stefano Papi

Translations from the Italian by Grace Crerar-Bromelow

First published in 2010 in hardcover in the United States of America by Thames & Hudson Inc., 500 Fifth Avenue, New York, New York 10110

thamesandhudsonusa.com

Library of Congress Catalog Card Number 2010923287

ISBN 978-0-500-51532-7

Printed and bound in China by C&C Offset Printing Co. Ltd

CONTENTS

Preface

The history and culture of imperial Russia have always held a deep fascination for me, in particular the court of the Romanovs, which was outstanding for its splendour and the elegance of its jewelry. In 1993, I had the opportunity to travel to St Petersburg with a group of colleagues from Sotheby's in London, where I was working at the time. The trip was organized by John Stuart, a great expert in Russian art and icons; his many stories, explanations and anecdotes embellished our guided tours of the imperial residences and brought back to life ghosts of a bygone era. I was totally captivated by what I saw and heard.

Since my trip to Russia my passion to research this fascinating subject had continued unabated, and over the years I have been able to build up an extensive archive of sale catalogues of the most important auction houses, as well as documents and images. Being a jewelry expert fortunate to have a good eye for recognizing pieces, I have at times been able to trace jewels back to the imperial court.

I will always be grateful to John for generously allowing me to share his boundless knowledge, and for his gifts of photographs and other materials which made valuable additions to my archive and were particularly useful in the creation of this book.

ABOVE: A diamond and pearl tiara belonging to the Mecklenburg-Strelitz family, sold at Christie's Geneva on 13 May 1981, identical to one from the Yusupov collection [262–63].

Introduction

The jewelry belonging to the Russian imperial crown constituted one of the most fabulous treasures of any European monarchy. By following the history of Nicholas II, the last Tsar, his family and his court, we can relive a time of great lavishness and power.

Jewelry has always played an important role in Russian culture. Folk headdresses in the shape of a halo, known as *kokoshniks*, for example, were traditionally covered with embroidered decoration which included coloured stones and beads. This custom was echoed in the imperial jewelry, with its *kokoshnik*-shaped tiaras which sparkled with the most beautiful stones that the Russian treasury could provide.

We will look at some of the most important jewels in the imperial collection, such as the regalia and *parures* created by the court jewellers for the last Tsarina; we will consider pieces belonging to Nicholas II's close family – his mother, the Dowager Empress Maria Feodorovna, and his sisters, Grand Duchesses Olga and Xenia; and through the collections of his extended family we will rediscover outstanding pieces such as the jewels that belonged to his aunt, Grand Duchess Vladimir.

The year 1909 saw the Ballets Russes in Paris, with dancers dressed in brightly coloured costumes designed by Leon Bakst which inspired a revolution in fashion and in colour schemes and inspired Oriental-themed soirées in Paris and St Petersburg. This period of light-heartedness was violently interrupted by the outbreak of the First World War, followed in 1918 by the end of the three-hundred-year-old Romanov dynasty.

The killing of the family of the last Tsar and the break-up of the ruling class were followed by the destruction of numerous collections of jewelry. While the beautiful collection of Grand Duchess Vladimir miraculously survived, and her diamond and pearl *kokoshnik* today belongs to the British Queen Elizabeth II, the Yusupov collection, secretly walled up in the family's palace, was discovered and almost entirely disassembled, the stones sold on the international market, and the settings melted down. In 1927, 140 pieces from the imperial collection, which the state had taken over, were sold at Christie's in London. Extraordinarily, many of the imperial jewels had been catalogued and photographed by the Soviet government, and we shall be able to draw on those illustrations.

We shall follow the fate of individual figures who subsequently lived in other European courts or in their beloved city of Paris, their jewelry often the only property the exiles were able to take with them in their flight. Still today pieces with this historic provenance appear occasionally on the international market, always creating great excitement.

The wedding of Princess Margrethe of Denmark and Prince René de Bourbon Parme in Copenhagen, on 9 June 1921. In the centre are the bride and bridegroom. To the left of them is the Duchess of Parma (the bridegroom's mother), and to the left of her the Dowager Empress Maria Feodorovna of Russia (the bride's aunt). Immediately behind these four figures, from left to right, are Prince George of Greece, Mademoiselle MacMahon, General MacMahon, Prince Valdemar of Denmark (the bride's father), Princess Isabella de Bourbon Parme and Princess George of Greece. At the back, from left to right, are Crown Prince Frederik of Denmark, Queen Alexandrine of Denmark (his mother), Princess Sixtus de Bourbon Parme, King Christian X of Denmark, Princes Felix and Sixtus de Bourbon Parme, Prince Axel, Grand Duchess Olga Alexandrovna of Russia (the bride's cousin), Princess Axel, Prince Erik, Princess Dagmar, Prince Louis de Bourbon Parme, an unknown, the Dowager Queen Louise of Denmark and Prince Xavier de Bourbon Parme.

Recollections of Romanovs

My mother, Princess Margrethe of Denmark, was the daughter of Prince Valdemar of Denmark and Princess Marie of Orléans. She was very close to her aunt, the Dowager Empress Maria Feodorovna, her father's sister. In 1909 when my grandmother, Princess Marie, became ill and her husband and older sons were on their way to the Far East, it was her sister-in-law, the Dowager Empress, on holiday in her native Denmark, who looked after her. My grandmother died, and after the funeral the Dowager Empress extended her stay for several months to look after my mother. My mother would often tell us about her trips to St Petersburg as a young girl, and the magnificence of that city. She also remembered the great care with which the Dowager Empress looked after the few jewels she had managed to take with her from Russia, reminders of her glorious past.

On 9 June 1921 Princess Margrethe married Prince René de Bourbon Parme in Copenhagen. The Dowager Empress Maria Feodorovna described the bride and groom – who were to be my parents – and the event in a letter of 15 June to her former governess, Sidonie L'Escaille:

> She was so pretty in her wedding dress and had a radiant air . . .
> the fiancé arrived with his mother, the Duchess of Parma. . . .
> The Duchess is charming. She is the sister of Archduchess Marie
> Thérèse, who was at our coronation in Moscow in 1883 and
> remembered it well. . . . Poor Valdemar was very moved. The bride
> is sweet and natural . . . From the church the young newlyweds
> drove together in a carriage . . . through the town lined with an
> immense crowd, who acclaimed them with cheers and threw
> flowers . . . We all followed in cars to the Amalienborg, where there
> was a gala lunch for the numerous guests in Christian VII's palace.

During the years when my mother's cousin, Grand Duchess Olga Alexandrovna, was living in Denmark, I saw her often. She was a magnificent person. She loved painting, and I still have a picture that she did of Bernstorff, my grandfather's summer palace where the family gathered every year, signed 'Olga'.

I wish you the best luck for your book –

Prince Michel de Bourbon Parme

9

~ 1 ~

THE LAST TSAR
AND HIS CLOSE FAMILY

In 1892, most of the members of the Russian imperial family were assembled for a party at Krasnoe Selo near St Petersburg, one of their summer residences, and were captured in a photograph [*opposite*].

In front, seated on the ground from left to right, are Grand Duke Alexei Mikhailovich, Grand Duke Michael Alexandrovich (youngest son of Alexander III), and Grand Dukes Andrei and Boris Vladimirovich.

The Emperor Alexander III and the Empress Maria Feodorovna are in the centre of the front row. To the right of the Emperor is Grand Duke Michael Nikolaievich; beyond him is the Emperor's youngest brother, Grand Duke Paul Alexandrovich. To the left of the Empress is Grand Duchess Alexandra Iosifovna (née Princess of Saxe-Altenburg), widow of Grand Duke Constantine Nikolaievich; she wears black for a recent bereavement, as does her daughter, Grand Duchess Olga Constantinovna (consort of George I, King of Greece), who stands behind her. At the left of the front row, from left to right, are Grand Duchess Xenia Alexandrovna (the Emperor's elder daughter); Maria Pavlovna, Grand Duchess Vladimir (née Duchess of Mecklenburg-Schwerin); and the latter's young daughter, Grand Duchess Elena Vladimirovna.

In the next row back, from left to right, are Duke Michael Georgievich of Mecklenburg-Strelitz; Duke George Georgievich of Mecklenburg-Strelitz; Grand Duke Constantine Constantinovich (brother of Queen Olga of Greece); Tsarevich Nicholas Alexandrovich – the future Tsar Nicholas II – behind his mother, the Empress; then Alexander III's brother Grand Duke Vladimir Alexandrovich; Alexander, Duke of Oldenburg; Grand Duke Dmitri Constantinovich; Peter, Duke of Oldenburg (who in 1901 was to marry Olga Alexandrovna, Alexander III's youngest child); and Prince George Maximilianovich Romanovsky, 6th Duke of Leuchtenberg. Standing at the very back are Grand Duke Sergei Mikhailovich and Grand Duke Nicholas Nikolaievich.

Grand Duke Alexander, the future Alexander III, had become Tsarevich after the death in 1865 of his older brother, Grand Duke Nicholas, and

Maria Feodorovna (left) with her sister, Alexandra, Princess of Wales, and their brother, Prince Valdemar of Denmark, *c.* 1885.

on 28 October 1866 he married his late brother's fiancée, Princess Dagmar of Denmark, familiarly known as 'Minny'. The two at once formed a close relationship, which was destined to last until his death in 1894. Four sons and two daughters were born from this happy union: Nicholas – the heir to the throne – in 1868; Alexander, who lived for only one year, in 1869; George in 1871; Xenia in 1875; Michael in 1878; and Olga in 1882.

In 1881, after the assassination of his father, Alexander at the age of only thirty-six found himself Emperor of All the Russias. The new Tsar moved with his family to the palace of Gatchina, some 65 kilometres

From the window of Fredensborg Castle in 1889, Queen Louise of Denmark looks down on her children: King George I of Greece; Empress Maria Feodorovna; Alexandra, Princess of Wales; Crown Prince Frederick; Thyra, Duchess of Cumberland; and Prince Valdemar.

(40 miles) south-east of St Petersburg, as it was much safer than the Winter Palace.

The Tsarina – who had taken the name of Maria Feodorovna – was the daughter of Christian IX of Denmark and Queen Louise (née Princess of Hesse-Kassel). All of King Christian's children made prestigious marriages: his daughter Alexandra married the Prince of Wales, the future King Edward VII; William took the crown of Greece under the name of George I in 1863; Dagmar became Tsarina of Russia; Thyra married Prince Ernest Augustus, 3rd Duke of Cumberland and Duke of Brunswick and Lunenburg; while his youngest son, Valdemar, refused the crown of Bulgaria, preferring instead to remain in Denmark and marry Princess Marie of Orleans.

ABOVE: A folding portable miniature-holder contain portraits of Alexander III and Maria Feodorovna's children and their dates of birth. (From left to right, they are Nicholas – the future Tsar Nicholas II – then George, Xenia, Michael and Olga.) Of gold and enamel, it was designed by Fabergé and executed by Michael Perkhin in St Petersburg before 1896. The rocaille decoration incorporating flowers and leaves is different on each of the five panels.

OPPOSITE: A portrait miniature of the Empress Maria Feodorovna by Zehngraf, bordered with pearls, set in a heart-shaped portable frame decorated with translucent red enamel designed by Fabergé and executed by Michael Perkhin, c. 1890. It was presented by the Tsarina as a Christmas gift to her sister Thyra, Duchess of Cumberland, in 1905.

Maria Feodorovna and Alexander III with their children – from left to right
the future Tsar Nicholas II, George (who died of tuberculosis in 1899), Xenia,
Olga, and, seated on the ground, Michael. They are seen at their residence
of Livadia in the Crimea in 1893.

An important diamond brooch of the Order of the White Eagle, *c.* 1880.
It was presented by Alexander III to a head of state, probably to be worn
at his coronation in 1883.

A magnificent *collier russe*, probably dating from the start of the 19th century,
in which Indian and Brazilian diamonds are mounted in gold and silver.
It could also be worn as a *tiare russe* [23], sewn onto a velvet *kokoshnik*;
each ray is individually numbered from 1 to 59, and has a hook at the back
to make the sewing easier.

A brooch with the initial of the Tsarina Maria Feodorovna surmounted by the imperial crown; it would have been worn by a lady-in-waiting in attendance, set against a blue ribbon of the Order of St Andrew.

The Emperor and Empress did not look favourably on the proposed marriage of Nicholas, the future tsar, to Alix of Hesse, the daughter of Princess Alice, a daughter of Queen Victoria, and Grand Duke Ludwig IV. Their attachment had begun in 1884, and Nicholas made no secret of it within his family. But she was a German princess, and Alexander III pressed his son to give up any hope of such a union, encouraged him to lead an active social life, and even looked favourably on his association with Mathilde Kschessinska, the prima ballerina of the Mariinsky Theatre in St Petersburg (see pp. 166–75).

Despite his relationship with Mathilde Kschessinska, Nicholas could not forget Princess Alix, and wrote in his diaries that he still dreamt of marrying her. Eventually, as Alexander III's health began to deteriorate, he asked that Alix be brought to Livadia so that he could extend his good wishes to her and bless her betrothal to his son – perhaps in acknowledgment that his son would soon ascend the throne. On 8 April 1894 Nicholas and Alix became officially engaged in Coburg Castle, on the occasion of the marriage of her brother, Ernst Ludwig of Hesse, to Princess Victoria Melita of Edinburgh, the granddaughter of Alexander II and niece of Alexander III. On 26 November, just one week after the state funeral of Alexander III, the wedding of Tsar Nicholas II and 'Alicky' – now Tsarina Alexandra Feodorovna – took place. It was the Dowager Empress Maria Feodorovna's birthday, and since in Russia one did not wear black on the monarch's birthday, the official mourning of the court was put aside. Most of the mourners who had come for the funeral stayed on for the wedding.

On the day of the wedding, the bride was accompanied by the Dowager Empress, who arrived at the Winter Palace from the residence of her brother-in-law, Grand Duke Sergei – Nicholas II's uncle, and husband of Alix's older sister, Grand Duchess Elizabeth. The imperial family waited in the Malachite Room of the palace. In this splendid space – decorated with malachite columns and fireplaces, complemented by red fabric-covered divans – the couple gathered and received the representatives of their families and the royal guests. The other guests made their way to the vast reception halls via the grand staircase, in a supreme display of elegant attire and sparkling jewelry. The royal cortege then proceeded to the palace chapel of SS. Peter and Paul. At the head of the procession, the Dowager Empress, clad in white, gave her arm to the King of Denmark. They were followed by the bridal couple, Nicholas in a red Hussars uniform, and Alexandra Feodorovna in a silver brocade dress with a long train carried by five officers of the court. Behind them

continued on page 26...

TOP AND ABOVE RIGHT: The coronet and brooch from the *parure* created for Tsarina Maria Feodorovna in the early 1880s [*see also* 22–23]. All the pearls, with outstanding lustre and shape, came from the repository of the Imperial Cabinet (see p. 62).

ABOVE LEFT: A brooch with a pearl encircled by perfectly colourless diamonds, from which are suspended a pink circular-cut diamond weighing 9 old carats and a rosy oval pearl surrounded by circular-cut diamonds of a yellowish hue.

ABOVE CENTRE: A bracelet with three strands of Oriental pearls; its clasp is made from an oval sapphire weighing more than 20 carats, encircled by diamonds.

ABOVE: The necklace, of diamonds and drop pearls, from the *parure* created
for Tsarina Maria Feodorovna in the early 1880s [*see* 22].

OPPOSITE, ABOVE: Tsarina Maria Feodorovna wearing the necklace, together
with a 19th-century brooch, several strings of pearls from the repository
of the Imperial Cabinet, and a typical diamond *tiare russe*.

RIGHT: The brooch worn by the Empress in her portrait, of the first half of the 19th century, is set with a rose-coloured oval-cut diamond, probably from the historic mines of Golconda in India, which weighs more than 17 old carats; it is encircled by twelve oval-cut diamonds weighing 24 old carats. The central pendant, a pear-shaped diamond weighing 28 old carats, is flanked by two pear-shaped diamonds each weighing 8 old carats; the purity and brilliance of the three stones suggest that they too are from Golconda. The setting is silver with gold channels.

Prince Henry
of Battenberg

Prince Philip
of Saxe-Coburg-Gotha

Prince Ferdinand
of Romania

Prince Henry
of Prussia

Prince Alfred,
Duke of Edinburgh
and of Saxe-Coburg-Gotha

Princess Louis
of Battenberg

Princess Philip of
Saxe-Coburg-Gotha

Princess Henry
of Battenberg

Duchess of
Connaught

Princess Henry
of Prussia

Grand Duke Sergei
Alexandrovich

Princess Beatrice of
Saxe-Coburg-Gotha

Prince Louis of Battenberg

Tsarevich Nicholas | Wilhelm II, Emperor of Germany | Grand Duke Vladimir Alexandrovich | Duke of Connaught | Princess Alexandra of Saxe-Coburg-Gotha | Edward, Prince of Wales

Grand Duchess Maria Alexandrovna of Russia, Duchess of Edinburgh and of Saxe-Coburg-Gotha | Princess Marie of Romania | Princess Alix of Hesse | Grand Duchess Vladimir | Princess of Saxe-Meiningen

Princess Elizabeth of Hesse, Grand Duchess Sergei | Prince Alfred of Saxe-Coburg-Gotha

Princess Feodora of Saxe-Meiningen

came the King of Greece with the Duchess of Saxe-Coburg-Gotha; the Grand Duke of Hesse with the Queen of Greece; the Duke of Saxe-Coburg-Gotha with the Princess of Wales; and the Prince of Wales with Princess Irene of Prussia.

In the chapel, the bride received holy water before the ceremony. The marriage was performed by the Metropolitan Archbishop, assisted by other Orthodox priests. Two gold crowns, adorned with medals ornamented with images of Christ and the Virgin Mary, were held above the heads of the bridal couple by several Russian grand dukes, who took turns to support the weight, while the Metropolitan stood in front of the imperial couple and held their hands under his stole. The crowns were then lowered, and the couple kissed the holy images of Christ and the Virgin. After the ceremony in the Winter Palace, on their way to the Anichkov Palace – the residence of the Dowager Empress Maria Feodorovna – the Tsar and Tsarina stopped on the Nevsky Prospekt, descended from their carriage, and entered the Kazan Cathedral, where in veneration they kissed the holy image of the Virgin.

The Dowager Empress presented her daughter-in-law with a magnificent necklace created by the court jeweller Bolin; it was made of five strands of pearls, the young Tsarina Alexandra's favourite jewel. Maria Feodorovna also commissioned a superb *parure* of sapphires and diamonds composed of a tiara, necklace and large brooch for Alexandra from the jeweller Friedrich Koechli.

On 3 November 1895 Alexandra gave birth to her first child, a girl, who was given the name Olga. In the same year, on 3 July, her sister-in-law, Grand Duchess Xenia, had given birth to her first child, Irina. Alexandra and Xenia were very fond of each other, and Nicholas's sister was probably the only member of the family who made an effort to understand the German princess, though eventually their relationship became more distant.

The coronation of Tsar Nicholas II and Tsarina Alexandra took place on 26 May 1896. It was accompanied by great festivities, and Nicholas ordered diamond brooches in the form of the Romanov imperial crown from the court jeweller Fabergé for the grand duchesses of the family.

The young Tsarina Alexandra Feodorovna, wearing a *tiare russe*, her favourite pearl necklaces, a diamond and pearl bow brooch, and the star of the Order of St Alexander Nevsky.

The ceremony, in the Cathedral of the Assumption in Moscow, began with a magnificent ritual, during which the Tsar received the crown from the hands of the Archbishop and placed it on his own head, a gesture which was symbolic of autocracy. The imperial crown [31] had been created in 1762 for Catherine the Great by the Swiss court jeweller Jérémie Pauzié (or Posier). He described its genesis in his memoirs:

LEFT AND BELOW: Two views of the coronation procession of Nicholas II in the Kremlin on 26 May 1896.

OPPOSITE: The moment in the coronation ceremony when the newly crowned Tsar Nicholas II crowns the Tsarina, Alexandra. His mother, the Dowager Empress Maria Feodorovna, stands at the left.

A few days after having ascended to the throne, Her Majesty
summoned me to tell me that she had instructed her chamberlain,
Monsieur de Betsky, to inspect the treasuries of the court.
Her Majesty asked me to melt down everything that no longer
seemed to be appropriate to modern taste. The resulting material
was to be used for a new crown that she wanted for her own
coronation. Her Majesty asked me to consult Monsieur de Betsky
on everything. I was delighted with this order, because it relieved

ABOVE: The cross and spinel from the imperial crown. The stone, weighing some 400 carats, was acquired in Peking (Beijing) in 1676 by the Russian Ambassador, Nicolae Milescu Spathari.

OPPOSITE: The great imperial crown, commissioned by Catherine the Great for her coronation in 1762 from the court jeweller Jérémie Pauzié (or Posier), and used for the coronation of all later members of the Romanov dynasty.

me of any responsibility which I might have had in relation to those who administered the treasury. I decided to accept completely and utterly the decisions of Monsieur de Betsky (who for his part was only desirous of realizing his own ambitions) and I contented myself with assisting him in everything that involved me. An excellent and well-qualified jewel-setter was recommended; he was a Frenchman by the name of Aurolé, and he carried out his work splendidly. From all the items I chose what was most suitable, and, as the Empress wanted the crown to remain unaltered after the coronation, I chose the largest stones – diamonds and coloured gems, which were not suitable for modern settings – and thus I created one of the richest objects that have ever existed in Europe. Despite the great care which we took to make the crown as light as possible, using only essential materials to fix the stones, in the end it still weighed five pounds [2.3 kg].

There is no record of the amount spent on the materials for this crown [*above and opposite*], since the precious stones belonged to the Treasury, but we know that Pauzié's invoice for all his work associated with the creation of this piece came to 50,000 roubles – a considerable sum, which was exceeded only by the cost of the entire ceremony. Aside from all the precious

Opposite: The imperial orb, in red gold, made by George Frederick Ekart in 1784, with diamond ornaments that look a generation earlier. In the centre is a magnificent antique pear-shaped Indian light blue diamond of 46.92 carats; at the top, below the diamond cross, is a 200-carat oval sapphire from Ceylon.

stones, a pound (0.5 kg) of gold and twenty pounds (9 kg) of silver were purchased for 86,000 roubles. From a series of portraits of Catherine the Great in which the royal insignia are represented, we can establish that the imperial crown remained almost unchanged to the present day.

The Tsar was then ready to receive the imperial orb and sceptre.

The orb [*opposite*] had been made by the jeweller George Frederick Ekart in 1784, apart from a large sapphire and diamond which were added at the end of the 18th century. It is of pure red gold, adorned with silver decorations and diamonds, which are assumed to be parts of other pieces of state-owned jewelry from the time of the Empress Elizabeth I Petrovna in the mid-18th century. The oval sapphire that surmounts it, weighing 200 carats, came from what was then Ceylon (now Sri Lanka); it is encircled with diamonds and supports a cross also set with diamonds. Where the decorative bands on the orb meet there is an antique diamond from the mines of Golconda, weighing 46.92 carats, which is a very pure stone with a light blue colour and very small fissures; its shape – it is a multi-faceted pear-shaped stone with a virtually flat base – is typical of antique Indian cuts.

The solid gold sceptre [35, 237] is composed of eight separate rings encircled by diamonds. The finial displays the historic Orlov diamond, weighing 189.62 carats, set in silver and bordered by diamonds. Above it is an imperial double eagle in black enamel, also decorated with diamonds; this eagle is detachable, and could be replaced with the emblem of Poland for particular ceremonial occasions. The Orlov diamond has a fascinating history. This Indian-cut stone is a fragment of a once much larger completely multi-faceted octahedron. It is clear and has a slight bluish-green tint. The diamond is named after Count Orlov, who presented it to Catherine the Great on her Saint's Day in 1774. The attendant festivities at Tsarskoe Selo were described in a letter a few days later by Count Solms, the Prussian Ambassador to the Russian court:

That day an enormous diamond imported from Persia was put on display; it had been deposited in the Bank of Amsterdam for some time, and had only recently been transferred to the Russian court. Prince Orlov acquired this jewel from the Armenian merchant Lazarev for the price of 400,000 roubles, and presented it to

Her Majesty, instead of a bouquet of flowers, on her Saint's Day. Her Majesty deigned to accept such a gift.

Legend relates that this exceptionally beautiful stone and another gem of equal value were once the eyes of an idol in South India, from which the diamond was stolen by a French soldier at the beginning of the 18th century. Nothing is known of its history until it appeared in the possession of Nadir Shah of Persia. After his death, the gem was evidently stolen once again, and ended up in the hands of Grigori Safras, a merchant from Julfa in Armenia: in a document dated 1768 a merchant called Guilianchev told Ivan Iakobi, Governor of Astrakhan, that Guilianchev's father-in-law, an Armenian merchant called Safras from Julfa, owned 'a rare treasure, a diamond of great value'. The prudent Armenian then brought this exceptionally precious jewel to Amsterdam, where he deposited it in a bank. In 1771 Safras drew up his will and instructed his heirs, the court jewellers Ivan and Iachim Lazarev, to 'take the diamond from East India weighing 770 Dutch ounces from the bank'. A year later Safras was still alive, and he finally sold the stone, reduced to half its size, to Ivan Lazarev for 125,000 roubles. Lazarev then sold the diamond to Count Orlov in 1774 at a price of 400,000 roubles, to be paid over seven years. Among surviving documents is one in which Lazarev requests that Safras's last will and testament be respected, and another in which he states that over the previous five years 11,800 roubles had been spent because of problems related to the sale of the stone. What these expenses involved is difficult to establish, but they almost certainly included the costs connected with the creation of a model of the stone sent to Catherine the Great in 1773. A document in the court offices dated 6 March 1773 records the following: 'paid to the banker Friederichs for a diamond, subsequently lost, and received together with the model of the great stone from Safras . . .' Whatever its precise history, the Orlov diamond became part of the Treasury of the Russian court in 1774 and since then it has adorned the finial of the sceptre.

As the coronation proceeded, Nicholas II signalled that the Tsarina was to approach him; this she did and, facing her husband, she knelt down on

OPPOSITE, LEFT: The top of the sceptre, where the historic Orlov diamond is surmounted by the imperial Romanov eagle. The diamond has an antique Indian cut; in 1914, following an examination by A. K. Fabergé, its weight was estimated to be 189.62 carats.

OPPOSITE, RIGHT: The sceptre seen in profile, and full length (59.5 cm/23½ in.).

a cushion in front of the throne. The Tsar removed his crown, placed it on his wife's head, and then replaced it on his own head. After this, he placed a much smaller crown on her head, which was fixed in place by four ladies-in-waiting. The Tsarina's small crown had been created by the jeweller Hahn from a model of the crown given as a dowry to the Dowager Empress, but it did not include diamonds taken from the imperial reserves. This little crown was made with stones from South Africa, provided by Hahn himself. The execution is extremely fine and the stones are matched perfectly. Now wearing her small crown, the Tsarina was invested with the Chain of St Andrew and the imperial cloak; the Tsar then embraced her, bade her rise from the prie-dieu, and invited her to sit on the throne next to him.

After the coronation ceremony, the first part of the communion service was celebrated. Nicholas II was accompanied by two archpriests for the anointing at the altar; as they walked, the chain of the Order of St Andrew [40, 41] worn by the Tsar slipped to the ground, which was interpreted as a bad omen. The Metropolitan Archbishop applied holy oil to the forehead, eyes, nostrils, mouth, ears, chest and hands of the Tsar, saying: 'This is the sign of the blessing of the Holy Spirit.' On the completion of the ritual, a gun salute was fired. The Tsarina now came forward and also received the holy oil, but only on her forehead.

The coronation with all its opulent celebrations concluded with a traditional feast for the people held in the Khodynka Meadow in Moscow. It was customary for the Tsar to order the distribution of handkerchiefs containing presents and tankards ornamented with the initials of the new Tsar and Tsarina and the Romanov coat of arms with its double eagle; free food and beer were also distributed to all.

From very early on the morning of 30 May 1896, more than five hundred thousand people had been gathering in the fields singing, dancing and making music, all expressing their delight at the coronation. Carts soon arrived loaded with food, beer and tankards which were to be distributed to everyone. Suddenly, at around six o'clock in the morning, a rumour spread that there would not be enough presents for everyone, and so the crowd began to run towards the wagons with the intention of securing the imperial gifts. Poor organization meant that this general

continued on page 42...

OPPOSITE: Tsar Nicholas II embraces his mother, the Dowager Empress Maria Feodorovna, after placing the crown on her head [*cf.* 38]. Standing at the left is Tsarina Alexandra. The image appeared in the *Illlustrated London News*, engraved after a drawing by the magazine's 'special artist in Moscow'.

THE CORONATION OF THE CZAR.—CONGRATULATIONS AFTER THE CROWNING CEREMONY: THE CZAR KISSING HIS MOTHER, THE DOWAGER EMPRESS.

Drawn by our Special Artist in Moscow.

OPPOSITE: The Dowager Empress Maria Feodorovna wearing the small imperial crown (above) for the coronation of Nicholas II. Her hair is styled in two long tresses that fall over her shoulders, as was stipulated by a court protocol for such occasions and for imperial weddings dating from the time of Catherine the Great.

ABOVE: The small imperial crown. Made of antique Indian and Brazilian diamonds, it was created in 1801 by the jeweller Louis David Duval. A document from the Imperial Cabinet notes: 'remit to the jeweller Duval 2,052 diamond stones for the sum of 37,854 rbls and 1212 cop. for the decoration of the crown of H. M. the Empress Elizabeth Alexeievna'. It rivals the larger imperial crown in its skilful execution and splendid stones.

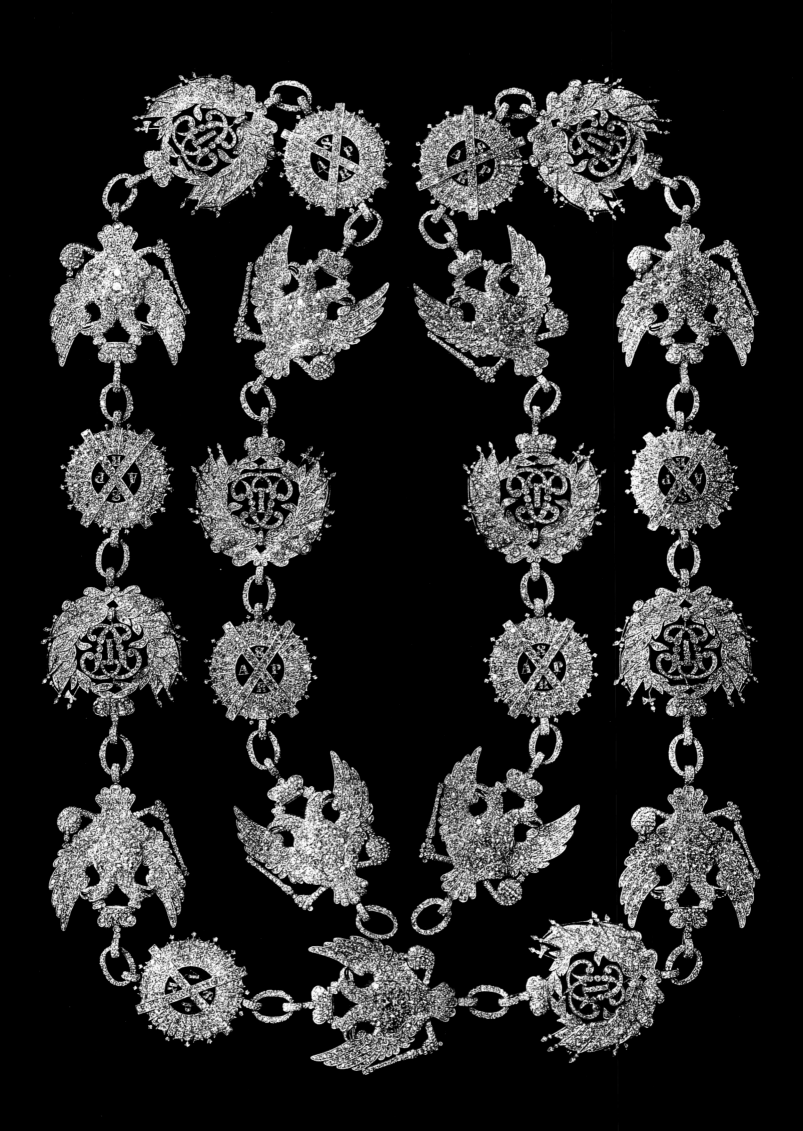

PRECEDING PAGES, LEFT: The centrepiece of the diamond chain of the Order of St Andrew. It is composed of twenty detachable elements, and includes the personal emblem of Paul I, Tsar from 1796 to 1801 (seen at the top).

PRECEDING PAGES, RIGHT: The small diamond chain of the Order of St Andrew, composed of twenty-three sections set with diamonds weighing more than 180 carats. Listed in an inventory of 1898 as dating from the time of Paul I, it was certainly created in the first half of the 19th century.

stampede could not be controlled, an so – according to official estimates – 1,400 people were crushed to death and 1,300 were injured; in reality the numbers were probably much higher.

The Tsar did not realize the seriousness of this disaster, and so allowed that day's festivities to continue. The only person to understand the true extent of the catastrophe was the Dowager Empress, Maria Feodorovna. She immediately ordered that a special commission of inquiry should be set up and that all other events should be cancelled, including a ball arranged for that evening in the French Embassy. Nicholas II's uncles, influenced by Grand Duke Sergei, Governor General of Moscow, persuaded him not to cancel the ball, in order not to offend the French. Grand Duchess Xenia later recalled that when the dancing began her husband, Grand Duke Alexander Mikhailovich, and his brothers left the ball in indignation. She remained, though she was shocked by the attitude of Grand Duke Sergei (for Sergei's part in the event see below, p. 86). The Dowager Empress was the only one to spend the night in the hospitals of Moscow comforting the injured and lending whatever practical support she could. In the following days, every injured person received a bottle of Madeira wine from her personally, and she also attended masses for the dead.

Although the Tsar paid for the funerals personally, the tragedy of the Khodynka Meadow was considered by the majority of the Russian people as a bad omen for the reign which had just begun.

The Tsar set up an inquiry led by Count Constantine Pahlen, a former Minister of Justice from the time of Alexander III and highly regarded by Maria Feodorovna, but he revoked this mandate when his uncle Sergei threatened to resign his governorship. The question of the actual responsibility for the terrible events in the Khodynka Meadow proved divisive. The Dowager Empress, along with most of the imperial family, blamed Grand Duke Sergei. On the other side, the young Tsarina Alexandra supported him, drawing criticism from the rest of the family. This was the beginning of the misunderstandings between the two empresses.

Subsequently, the division between the empresses became ever more marked because of a law of 1797, enacted by Paul I, which gave the

Dowager Empress precedence over the wife of the Tsar at official functions – unlike the practice in all other European monarchies. Thus, Maria Feodorovna would take the arm of the Tsar, while Tsarina Alexandra had to take the arm of one of the oldest grand dukes.

Another controversy arose over the crown jewels: according to protocol, these had to be passed from the Dowager Empress to the reigning Tsarina. Maria Feodorovna, however, refused to comply, and even an intercession from Nicholas II seemed at first to be fruitless. In the end, on the insistence of the Tsar, who invoked the tradition that the wife of the Tsar was entitled to wear certain jewels belonging to the Imperial Treasury on particular state occasions, the Dowager Empress relented, although she retained some of the most important jewels for her own personal use.

On 10 June 1897 a second daughter, Tatiana, was born, followed by a third daughter, Maria, on 26 June 1899. On 18 June 1901 a fourth daughter was born – Anastasia, to the great disappointment of the Tsarina, anxious to give birth to an heir to the dynasty.

In 1903 the Bal des Costumes Russes or Russian Costume Ball took place in the Winter Palace, one of the most famous masquerade balls ever held there. It was held to celebrate the bicentenary of the founding of St Petersburg, but Nicholas II, whose passion for the era of the 17th-century Tsar Alexis I was well known, required his guests to come dressed in costume of that time. The preparations occupied the court for several months. The event itself was held on two days. The first day, 11 February, began with a concert in the theatre of the Hermitage, at which the greatest artists of the time performed, including Chaliapin and Anna Pavlova. This was followed by a dinner in the Hermitage and much later by a ball in the Pavilion Hall which finished at two o'clock in the morning. At this event there were 390 guests. On 13 February a smaller, select group of 250 people gathered in the Winter Palace for what was remembered as the Grand Ball. Tsarina Alexandra, Grand Duchess Xenia Alexandrovna and Grand Duchess Vladimir were among the guests, recorded in their special costumes and lavish jewelry [47, 66, 101]. Grand Duke Alexander Mikhailovich later recalled that this was the last spectacular ball held in the Russian Empire.

In August 1904 the heir to the throne, Tsarevich Alexei, was born. The infant soon showed the symptoms of haemophilia, a terrible disease which was carried by the daughters and granddaughters of Queen Victoria. For Tsarina Alexandra, a granddaughter of Queen Victoria, the illness of her baby was a blow which served to isolate her further from the family and the rest of the court. The infant Tsarevich's haemophilia was kept secret.

continued on page 53...

ABOVE: A coronet, from a magnificent *parure* commissioned by Tsarina
Alexandra Feodorovna in 1900 from the court jewellers Bolin and Fabergé.
The *parure* was set with large cabochon emeralds and diamonds – the
diamonds from South Africa; all the pieces were mounted in silver with gold
galleries, and all the elements were numbered so they could be taken apart.
The coronet and the necklace [296] were made in great haste by the jeweller
Schwerin in the firm of Bolin. The coronet was set with a large quadrangular
sugarloaf cabochon emerald of rare beauty, weighting about 23 carats.
(The *devant de corsage*, with the same bow design, set with five exceptional
cabochon emeralds, was made by the jeweller Oscar Piel in the Moscow
branch of Fabergé.)

OPPOSITE: The Tsarina seen wearing the coronet, in her portrait painted
in 1907 by N. K. Bodarevsky.

ABOVE: A *collier d'esclave* necklace created for the Empress Alexandra to wear at the Bal des Costumes Russes or Russian Costume Ball, held in the Winter Palace in St Petersburg in 1903. Fabergé made it in a great hurry, using the most beautiful stones in the imperial collection – emeralds from the Ural Mountains mounted in gold and Brazilian diamonds set in silver (all mounted on silver wire for flexibility).

OPPOSITE, RIGHT: The Empress dressed for the ball. She wears the *collier d'esclave* by Fabergé seen above, and, suspended from it, an enormous cabochon emerald weighing 250 carats, dating from the time of Nicholas I. The emerald – thought to be one of the first gems found in the Urals, *c.* 1835 – with a semi-cabochon convex face and a multi-faceted base was mounted in gold and bordered with diamonds which, in turn, were mounted in silver. Her dress is a copy of one that belonged to Maria Ilyinichna, the wife of the 17th-century Tsar Alexei Mikhailovich. It is modelled on a *platno*, an old Russian style of coat with wide sleeves, which was worn on special occasions such as festivals and ceremonies.

OPPOSITE, LEFT: The chain that adorned the Empress's headscarf, made of polished ovoid elements encrusted with diamonds alternating with pearls and terminating in two tassels fringed with Brazilian pear-shaped diamonds. The entire piece is mounted in silver. A particularly fine example of late 18th-century jewelry, it has been attributed to the famous St Petersburg jeweller Jean-Jacques Duc.

OVERLEAF, LEFT AND RIGHT: A portrait of the Empress Alexandra by Friedrich August von Kaulbach shows her wearing the tiara from the diamond and sapphire *parure* shown opposite. It was designed for her at the beginning of the 20th century by Friedrich Koechli, a Swiss jeweller in St Petersburg, who became court jeweller in 1902. The tiara has a design of intertwined semicircles in which sixteen large sapphires are set, mounted in gold with a small gold channel; the diamonds are mounted in silver and linked with gold. Shown with it is the matching *devant de corsage*.

ABOVE AND OPPOSITE, TOP: The Empress Alexandra wearing an exceptional tiara in the form of a *kokoshnik*. Created at the beginning of the 19th century, it belonged to Tsarina Elizabeth Alexeievna, consort of Alexander I. It is set with antique Brazilian diamonds with an approximate weight of 275 old carats, mounted in gold and silver.

OPPOSITE, BELOW: A diamond bracelet by the St Petersburg jeweller Johann Wilhelm Keibel, mid-19th century. The clasp has three large diamonds with a total weight of more than 15 carats, bordered by circular brilliant-cut diamonds. The four strands of antique-cut diamonds mounted in silver with a gold channel are held together by silk thread for maximum flexibility. This bracelet was worn by Romanov brides on their wedding day.

Below: The Dowager Empress Maria Feodorovna, painted in 1905 by Emil O. Vizel. She is wearing the *collier d'esclave* necklace seen opposite.

Opposite: This exceptional *collier d'esclave* is formed of a string of twenty-one cushion-cut diamonds, mounted in silver settings with a channel in gold below held together by silk threads to make the necklace more flexible. Suspended from this are fifteen antique pear-shaped diamonds, each surmounted by a much smaller diamond: probably cut some time in the 17th or 18th century, they are of Indian origin and have a total weight of 475 old carats. Some of the diamonds have a blue or pink tint, producing an enchanting effect. The central stone in the string weighs about 32 carats; the stones on either side weigh between 23 and 16 carats; the central pear-shaped diamond weighs 26 carats; and the four flanking it weigh between 25 and 16 carats.

The year 1905 saw great and painful events. Repeated defeats by Japan had created a highly unstable situation, with civil unrest at home. What came to be known as the 1905 Revolution effectively began on 22 January. Father George Gapon, a spiritual authority for the striking workers, had planned a peaceful march on which he was to carry a petition to the Winter Palace demanding a constituent assembly, a reduction in working hours, freedom of religion and expression, and an amnesty for political prisoners. The march had been authorized by the police and by the Tsar himself, who was then living in the Alexander Palace in Tsarskoe Selo. However, on the evening before the march, Nicholas announced that he had decided not to accept the demonstrators' petition. Maintenance of public order had been entrusted to the police, who requested the assistance of the army. The procession moved calmly and peacefully, workers, women and children carrying icons and portraits of the Tsar – but as they approached the Winter Palace the troops fired on them, leaving some thousand people dead and wounded. The day is known in Russian history as 'Bloody Sunday'. After the tragedy, the government advised the Tsar to make a gesture to comply with the popular demands. Grand Duke Sergei, Governor General of Moscow, was totally intransigeant. Seeing that a softer

LA MANIFESTATION DU 31 OCTOBRE A SAINT-PÉTERSBOURG. — A L'UNIVERSITÉ

line was being taken towards the demands of the workers, he resigned, and moved out of the Governor's Palace. He did, however, return there regularly, a pattern that allowed an anarchist to throw a bomb into his carriage and kill him on 17 February (see pp. 86–87 and 92). Unrest continued; on 31 October in St Petersburg, university students organized a demonstration against the government. In that month the creation of the Duma, an elective constituent assembly that could receive petitions from the people, was announced. The Duma first met in May the following year.

One of the most important figures of the imperial family during these years was Grand Duke Nicholas Nikolaievich, a cousin of Alexander III, known in the family as Nikolasha. In 1907 he married Princess Anastasia Petrovich Njegosh of Montenegro (she became Grand Duchess Anastasia Nikolaievna), whose previous marriage to Prince George Maximilianovich, 6th Duke of Leuchtenberg, had been annulled in 1906. Her sister Militza had married Nikolasha's brother, Grand Duke Peter Nikolaievich, in 1889. The two Grand Duchesses were to introduce the baleful figure of the monk Rasputin to Tsarina Alexandra (see p. 222).

In October 1912 Nicholas II's brother, Grand Duke Michael Alexandrovich, married Natasha Wulfert, with whom he had long enjoyed a relationship and had a son, George, in 1910. Maria Feodorovna, who had tried unsuccessfully to find a bride for her son among the European royal families, was shattered by the news: Natasha was not only a commoner, but twice divorced. The son that she had seen as a successor, should the illness of the Tsarevich get worse, was deprived of his title and fortunes and exiled from Russia. (Eventually he was allowed to return.)

In 1913 the Romanov dynasty celebrated its tercentenary. There was a procession through cheering crowds in St Petersburg, a performance of *A Life for the Tsar* at the Mariinsky Theatre, and a magnificent ball – at which Alexandra caused resentment by leaving early.

The season of 1914 was the most brilliant ever. Great events followed one another, each ball more resplendent than the last. The Dowager Empress organized a ball for her granddaughters Olga and Tatiana in the Anichkov Palace. This was the last glittering event held there before the outbreak of the First World War.

OPPOSITE: University students demonstrating against the government in St Petersburg on 31 October 1905.

OPPOSITE: The Empress Alexandra in court dress for the opening of the first Duma in 1906, photographed by K. Bulla. She wears the diadem seen above, a small diamond chain of the Order of St Andrew, and a *collier de chien* in pearls and diamonds and a pearl and diamond cluster necklace, both surely created by Bolin to accompany the diadem. Neither necklace appears among the inventoried jewels, and it is likely that they had been taken by the Empress to Tobolsk and then disappeared.

ABOVE: This splendid diadem, worn by the Empress Alexandra at the opening of the Duma, was catalogued by Fersman as early 19th century, but it is more likely to have been made by the court jeweller Bolin expressly for the Tsarina, using antique pearls and diamonds from the Imperial Cabinet. Fersman considered it to be the finest piece in the entire imperial collection. All trace of it is lost after the inventory of 1922, and it seems likely that as with other pieces from the collection it was sold or broken up when some of the imperial jewels were sold by Christie's in London in 1927.

OVERLEAF: Nicholas II reading the inaugural statement of the first Duma in St George's Hall in the Kremlin on 11 May 1906. Standing at the far left are the Dowager Empress Maria Feodorovna with her daughters Xenia and Olga, the Empress Alexandra, and Grand Duchess Vladimir.

ABOVE: Pieces from the second half of the 18th century, including solid silver flowers typical of the decorations which were sewn onto the clothes of several empresses. In the centre are aigrettes set with diamonds and pearls.

OPPOSITE: A series of such flowers is sewn on the black velvet ribbon worn round her neck by the Dowager Empress Maria Feodorovna, seen playing cards in the Amalienborg Palace in Copenhagen with her sisters, Queen Alexandra of Great Britain and Thyra, Duchess of Cumberland, and her brother, Frederick VIII of Denmark.

Grand Duchess Xenia

The future Tsar Nicholas II's sister Xenia Alexandrovna, the eldest daughter of Alexander III and Maria Feodorovna, was born on 25 March 1875 in the Anichkov Palace in St Petersburg, and christened in the chapel of the Winter Palace on 17 April (the birthday of her grandfather, Alexander II); her godparents were her grandmother, Tsarina Maria Alexandrovna, her grandfather, King Christian IX of Denmark, her uncle, Grand Duke Vladimir Alexandrovich, and her mother's younger sister, Princess Thyra of Denmark. She grew into a very pretty young woman, with beautiful eyes like her mother's. Prince Felix Yusupov, later her son-in-law, commented: 'her chief attraction lay not in her beauty but in the rare delicate charm which she had inherited from her mother, the Empress'.

In the summer of 1894 Alexander III experienced one of the happiest moments in the final months of his life: the marriage of Xenia to Grand Duke Alexander Mikhailovich, the son of Grand Duke Michael Nikolaievich – grandson of Nicholas I – and Princess Cecilie of Baden (Olga Feodorovna). The wedding took place in Peterhof, a splendid palace overlooking the Gulf of Finland. It was to be one of the last times when the crown commissioned a true 'treasury' of jewelry: the Tsar and Tsarina ordered four complete *parures* for their daughter (the historian Alexander von Solodkoff discovered the original designs for them, complete with inscriptions, more than ten years ago, and was able to authenticate them with the assistance of a descendant of Grand Duchess Xenia). Several years before the wedding, in January 1889, Alexander III had visited the repository of the Imperial Cabinet to select the emeralds. (The Imperial Cabinet had been established in the reign of Peter the Great, and finally restructured by Alexander II in 1884–93. It was the most important administrative institution of the court. One of its main tasks was the care of the imperial jewels, and payment for purchases ordered by the tsar and for goods supplied to the court. Here the most beautiful loose stones, collected over many years by the different tsars, which belonged to the Treasury, were kept.) Following Alexander III's visit, the Minister of the Court commissioned three jewellers, Fabergé, Bolin and Ewing, each to design a *parure*, and the Tsar then chose the design to be executed.

In the summer of the wedding, Nicholls and Ewing of Nevsky Prospekt created a spectacular *parure* of emeralds and diamonds [264]. This consisted of a necklace, formed of a series of oval and rectangular cabochon emeralds, each surrounded by circular-cut diamonds, and from each of which hung a pear-shaped cabochon emerald; a coronet with a floral design entirely set with diamonds supporting pear-shaped cabochon emeralds;

and a large brooch with cabochon emeralds, mounted in a double ring of diamonds, which could also be a centrepiece in the necklace. An inscription on the preparatory designs reads: 'From papa and mama on the wedding'.

At the same time, Bolin worked on an important commission from Tsarina Maria Feodorovna to create a *parure* consisting of a tiara, necklace and large brooch in diamonds and rubies [265]. The stones, which were especially rare and carefully matched in colour, also came from the repository of the Imperial Cabinet. Their selection was entrusted to Bolin with the collaboration of Ewing.

Grand Duchess Xenia and her husband, Grand Duke Alexander Mikhailovich, in their palace in St Petersburg with their seven children – from left to right Nikita, Irina, Andrei, Dmitri, Vasily (on his mother's lap), Fyodor and Rostislav.

Grand Duchess Xenia's parents also presented her with two large diamond *rivière* necklaces and a wonderful tiara, also created by Bolin, entirely decorated with briolette-cut diamonds which quivered with every movement of the head. There was also a diamond brooch that included three pear-shaped diamonds reminiscent of some owned by the Empress [265]. Her parents' gifts were completed by a *parure* of cabochon sapphires and diamonds (it has not proved possible to discover which atelier made this) and a five-stranded pearl *collier de chien* with a large button pearl clasp.

The bridegroom, Grand Duke Alexander Mikhailovich, presented Xenia with a splendid *collier russe* in diamonds [265], with the message: 'From Sandro on our wedding'. Designed by Bolin, this could also be worn as a tiara. It was accompanied by a brooch with a naturalistic design of two vine leaves in diamonds which supported a drop cabochon emerald. The brooch was later given by Xenia to her daughter, Princess Irina, when she married Prince Felix Yusupov in 1914.

(Alexander III also offered his daughter another wedding present, the Mikhailovsky Palace, in the centre of St Petersburg close to the Nevsky Prospekt, but the youthful Grand Duchess found it too imposing, and chose instead the palace of Countess Vorontsov on the bank of the Moika Canal, which was decorated to her specifications within a year.)

In accordance with imperial tradition, Xenia wore the wedding jewelry that had been worn by the preceding grand duchesses of the Romanov dynasty [51, 53, 249–51]. Also following tradition, she wore a splendid silver brocade dress with a long train and long Muscovite style sleeves that left her arms free, all decorated with gold and silver embroidery. Ladies-in-waiting had to wear a *kokoshnik*, a traditional Russian headdress in the shape of a tiara, usually made of cloth, adorned with jewelry: theirs were of plain velvet bordered with pearls. (Towards the end of the 19th century, women of the imperial family chose to wear tiaras in a similar shape created by the most important jewellers of the period, such as Fabergé and Bolin in Russia and Cartier, Chaumet and Boucheron in France, and these came to be known as *kokoshniks* [*e.g.* 50–51, 114–17].)

Over her wedding dress, Xenia wore a crimson velvet cloak with an ermine collar held in place by a large diamond clasp that had belonged to Catherine the Great. Her hair was arranged so that two long tresses hung down over her shoulders. On her head she wore the tiara that had belonged to Tsarina Elizabeth Alexeievna, consort of Tsar Alexander I, and above that her nuptial crown. Around her neck was an enormous *collier d'esclave* necklace. She also wore earrings decorated with two large diamonds and a bracelet with three strands of brilliant-cut diamonds.

The bridegroom, on the other hand, wore his naval uniform.

LEFT: Grand Duchess Xenia in the centre, flanked by her mother, the Dowager Empress Maria Feodorovna, and brother, Grand Duke Michael, and two of her sons.

BELOW: Grand Duchess Xenia at her desk, in her house in the Crimea.

PRECEDING PAGES, LEFT: Grand Duchess Xenia dressed in boyar costume for the Bal des Costumes Russes given by the Tsar in the Winter Palace in 1903 (see p. 43). On her dress she wears the jewelry that she had received from her parents on her wedding. Around her neck her two diamond *rivière* necklaces are arranged as a *collier de chien*, with a string of large white Oriental pearls in the centre, and she also wears the *collier russe* given to her by her husband as a wedding present. Her cabochon emerald and diamond necklace has a large emerald and diamond brooch as a centrepiece, and alternating with its cabochon emerald drops are sections of a diamond and ruby necklace. The cabochon emeralds from the tiara in the *parure* with the necklace are sewn onto her headdress. Other precious stones are sewn into the embroidery on the snow-white brocade of her dress. In her hand she holds the feather fan seen opposite.

PRECEDING PAGES, RIGHT: The feather fan designed by Fabergé for Grand Duchess Xenia to carry at the ball. It has a gold disc covered with translucent pink guilloché enamel to hold the feathers, and a rock crystal handle.

The wedding procession passed through the salons of the Peterhof Palace to the Cathedral of SS. Peter and Paul. A twenty-one-gun salute marked the entrance of the Tsar and Tsarina at the head of a long procession of members of the imperial family in a precise order of precedence. Guests were given a memento of the event: Hahn, the St Petersburg jewellers, designed cufflinks for the gentlemen guests, with a diamond-encircled portrait miniature of the bride on one link and of the groom on the other, while the ladies each received two buttons with the same decoration.

The bridal couple spent their wedding night at Ropsha, one of the residences of the Vladimirs. The following day a gala event was organized in the couple's honour in the imperial theatre of the Peterhof Palace. The theatre had been completely restored and enlarged, supplied with electric light, and decorated splendidly for the occasion. The ballet corps of the Mariinsky Theatre in St Petersburg performed the première of *Le Réveil de Flore* ('The Awakening of Flora'), with music by Riccardo Drigo and choreography by Marius Petipa. The role of Flora was danced by the prima ballerina of the Mariinsky Theatre, Mathilde Kschessinska (see pp. 166–75) – the first love and former mistress of Xenia's brother, the Tsarevich.

Xenia's marriage and the celebrations of her wedding were the last great occasion in which Maria Feodorovna took part as the reigning empress. Just a few months later, Alexander III was dead, leaving his son to become tsar as Nicholas II.

OPPOSITE: An official photograph of Grand Duchess Xenia, taken in 1916.

Grand Duchess Olga

The younger sister of Nicholas and Xenia, Grand Duchess Olga Alexandrovna, was born in the Peterhof Palace on 13 June 1882. A free spirit, as she grew up Olga preferred to devote herself to her favourite pastimes – music (she played the violin) and art (she was a talented painter), and taking long walks in the open air of the parks – rather than spend her time in the social swirl of grand receptions. Unlike her mother, she was no great lover of fashion or jewelry: she would wear only a few strings of pearls, lent to her by her mother, and that only when she was obliged to be present on official occasions. Above all, Olga loved her country and completely rejected any idea of a possible marriage to a foreign husband who would take her away from Russia.

In May 1901, her engagement to Prince Peter, Duke of Oldenburg, was announced. He was fourteen years her senior, and the only son of Alexander, Duke of Oldenburg and Duchess Eugenie Maximilianovna, Princess Romanov, Duchess of Oldenburg. Peter was aide-de-camp to the Tsar and held the rank of lieutenant in the Preobrazhensky Regiment.

It is said that the Tsar was particularly fond of his young sister, and on the occasion of her marriage, celebrated on 9 August 1901 in the palace of Gatchina in the presence of their closest relatives, he presented her with gifts that included a wonderful fan created by Fabergé [74]. It had a central image of the imperial couple receiving bread and salt in accordance with ancient tradition, surrounded by gold decoration covered in translucent yellow enamel and diamonds; on one side the Grand Duchess's monogram alternated with a double-headed eagle in diamonds, while the other side was decorated with heart-shaped diamonds and the date of the wedding, also written in diamonds. Their union was not consummated. Olga suffered this loveless bond uncomplainingly, not even mentioning it to her mother, and accepted her situation with great dignity.

The young Grand Duchess was idolized by her people, who appreciated her human qualities and her simplicity of spirit. General Alexander Spiridovich tells a story in his book, *Les Dernières Années de la cour de Tsarskoïe-Sélo* ('The Last Years of the Court at Tsarskoe Selo'), published in 1928:

> Shortly after my appointment in 1906, an incident made a great impression on me. I had a visit one day from one of my men, Yurkov, who, as he invited me to his wedding, told me that his sponsor was Grand Duchess Olga Alexandrovna and his best man was Colonel Komarov, the commander of my battalion.

The wedding was to take place in the church of the Fourth Battalion
of Imperial Archers, and as they were commanded by the Duke
of Oldenburg, the Grand Duchess's husband, it was she who was
in charge of organizing the ceremony. I had not known such
unaffectedness in many members of the imperial family, and I was
shocked that the sister of the Tsar was a witness for the marriage of
a lower-ranking officer in the reserve, a mere member of the guard.
This seemed incredible to me, so I started to ask Yurkov lots of
questions, and learnt that the imperial family took a great interest

Grand Duchess Olga, wearing a string of pearls with a large drop pearl.

in their soldiers, the lower-ranking officers of the battalion of the guard and His Majesty's escort when they were in service guarding the palace. The sovereign and his family would often ask them about their personal and family circumstances, about their parents whom they had left behind in their villages, and often provided them with financial assistance. One day, Grand Duchess Olga had said to Yurkov: 'When you decide to get married, invite me to your

Grand Duchess Olga with her husband, Peter, Duke of Oldenburg.

wedding', and so she had offered to be the witness to his marriage. For me, as a young officer from the provinces, all this seemed bizarre, if not unreal. The day appointed for Yurkov's wedding came, it was held in the church of the Imperial Archers, and the bride was a simple peasant girl from the village of Kurmino. Indeed, all the guests came from that little village. After the benediction, a reception was held in a small room inside the church. Fruit, champagne and sweets were served. The Grand Duchess was so unaffected and kindly, and talked in such a familiar way to the bride and her family, that if a stranger had witnessed this scene, he would never have believed that it was the sister of the Emperor of All the Russias before him.

In 1903, the young Grand Duchess had an encounter which was destined to change the course of her life. On the occasion of a military parade at Gatchina, Olga saw her brother, Grand Duke Michael, talking to a young officer who belonged to the same regiment. He was the charming Nikolai Kulikovsky. For Olga, it was love at first sight. The next day, Grand Duke Michael invited his sister and Kulikovsky to dinner, and the officer showed the same interest in the young Grand Duchess as she did in him. Although he was descended from an eminent military family, Nikolai Kulikovsky had no noble title. Olga wanted to divorce her husband at once, but this would have provoked malicious rumours, and as she would be marrying a person of a lesser rank, she would have to leave Russia. Despite this, Olga and Kulikovsky started to see each other regularly, especially at Gatchina, which was the location of his regimental headquarters. The Dowager Empress was determined to avoid scandal at all costs, and so, to save appearances, the young Kulikovsky was appointed as aide-de-camp to Duke Peter, and he came to live at their residence in Sergievskaya Street. For Maria Feodorovna, the fact that her young daughter was living under the same roof as her husband and lover was a source of great displeasure, but it was preferable to a divorce.

At the outbreak of war Kulikovsky's regiment was going to be one of the first to be sent to the front: on hearing the news, Olga decided to leave her husband for good. She returned the jewelry given her by the Oldenburg family and entrusted her own pieces to her loyal maid, Mimka. She became a nurse at an army hospital in Kiev, and there, in the course of a visit, her brother the Tsar gave her permission to divorce her husband. She and Nikolai Kulikovsky were married on 5 November 1916 in a ceremony which was attended by her mother, Maria Feodorovna.

ABOVE: Grand Duchess Olga in court dress, in 1908. She wears a *tiare russe* on a fabric *kokoshnik*, and around her neck large diamond *rivières* from the Imperial Cabinet, lent to her, together with the *devant de corsage*, by her mother. She holds a fan of enamel and diamonds by Fabergé, one of the wedding gifts from her brother, Nicholas II.

OPPOSITE: *Rivières* from the Imperial Cabinet, composed of Indian diamonds set in silver with gold galleries. According to Fersman's catalogue, the central stone of the longest *rivière* came from the mines at Golconda, and was of light blue colour.

~2~

ROMANOV RELATIONS

Alexander III was survived by his four brothers and his sister. Eldest was Grand Duke Vladimir Alexandrovich (1847–1909), who had married Marie, Duchess of Mecklenburg-Schwerin. From them the Vladimirovich branch is descended (see pp. 94–129).

Vladimir was followed by Grand Duke Alexei Alexandrovich (1850–1908), who remained unmarried, though from an early affair he had a son. Alexei impressed people as an elegant and athletic figure, with infinite charm. Grand Admiral of the Russian navy, he was one of the organizers of the circumnavigation of Africa and Asia by the fleet under Admiral Rodjestvensky's armada; that ended disastrously with the attack on the Japanese fleet at Tsushima in 1905 which led to Japan's victory in the Russo-Japanese War and put an end to his career. He later moved to Paris [205], and died there.

Next came Grand Duchess Maria Alexandrovna (1853–1920), who married Prince Alfred, Duke of Edinburgh, second child of Queen Victoria and Prince Albert of Saxe-Coburg-Gotha (see pp. 77–85).

Grand Duke Sergei Alexandrovich (1857–1905) married Princess Elizabeth of Hesse, sister of the future Empress Alexandra Feodorovna, and had no children (see pp. 86–93).

Youngest was Grand Duke Paul Alexandrovich (1860–1919), who was first married to Princess Alexandra of Greece, with whom he had two children, and after her early death to Olga von Pistohlkors, with whom he had three more children (see pp. 130–43).

We shall first meet Grand Duchess Maria and Grand Duke Sergei.

Grand Duchess Maria and her Family

In the summer of 1868, while visiting the German town of Jugenheim, the young Prince Alfred, Duke of Edinburgh, second son of Queen Victoria, met Grand Duchess Maria Alexandrovna (1853–1920), Tsar Alexander II's beloved only daughter, for the first time. When he returned to England, 'Affie' (as he was called by his family) told his mother of his intention to marry the young Grand Duchess. The Queen was not at all pleased by this news, not only because Britain and Russia had been enemies ever since the Crimean War, but also for religious reasons.

Nevertheless, in 1871 Affie travelled to Russia, and, following his visit, the Tsar wrote to Queen Victoria indicating that he was favourably disposed to an engagement between his daughter and the Duke of Edinburgh. The young lovers continued to find that they had much in common, and they both adored music, in particular the piano, although Affie also played the violin. Another two years passed before the engagement became official, in July 1873. An agreement was reached between the British Queen and the Russian Tsar that any offspring of their children would be brought up in the Protestant religion.

The couple were married on 23 January 1874 in the chapel of the Winter Palace, in a double ceremony. The Orthodox ritual was performed first, by the metropolitan bishops of St Petersburg, Moscow and Kiev, in which Grand Dukes Vladimir, Alexei and Sergei and the bridegroom's brother, Prince Arthur, took turns in holding golden crowns above the heads of the bridal couple. The Church of England ceremony was then conducted by Arthur Stanley, Dean of Westminster. Queen Victoria was represented by the Prince and Princess of Wales. For his beloved daughter, Tsar Alexander II commissioned a spectacular complete *parure* of rubies and diamonds from the court jeweller Bolin [78–79]. Other fabulous pieces of jewelry that he gave her included a magnificent *tiare russe* made of diamonds which could also be worn as a necklace [80–81].

There were five children of the marriage: Alfred, born in 1874; Marie in 1875; Victoria Melita in 1876; Alexandra in 1878; and Beatrice in 1884. Of the four daughters, the most beautiful and fascinating was Marie, with a classic figure, splendid blonde hair and blue eyes, and an innate elegance. She married Prince Ferdinand of Hohenzollern-Sigmaringen, a member of the Catholic branch of the Hohenzollern family and heir to the throne of Romania, in Sigmaringen Castle on 10 January 1893. (Because her future husband was a Catholic, she lost her right of succession to the British throne as Queen Victoria's granddaughter.)

continued on page 84...

The *parure* seen on these two pages was ordered by
Alexander II from the court jeweller Bolin for the marriage
in 1874 of his daughter Maria Alexandrovna to Prince
Alfred, Duke of Edinburgh. It comprised a diamond
coronet decorated with floral motifs with ruby centres;
a necklace of cushion-cut diamonds alternating with
rubies, also cushion-cut; a bangle with twelve cushion-cut
diamonds of ever increasing size centred on a Burmese
ruby weighing 8.40 carats; a ring with a cushion-cut ruby
of 9.19 carats; a pair of earrings; and a large brooch –
originally the centrepiece of a *devant de corsage* – with
a central oval ruby weighing more than 12 carats. All the
stones are consistent in colour and of the finest quality.

Maria, Duchess of Edinburgh and Saxe-Coburg-Gotha, wearing the *tiare russe*
shown opposite, together with several strings of Oriental pearls and a pearl
and diamond brooch with an important drop pearl.

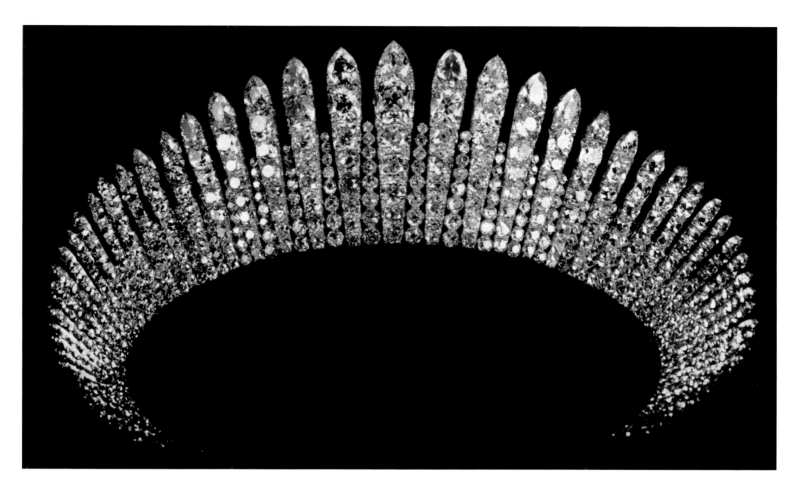

A splendid diamond *tiare russe*, one of the gifts presented by Alexander II to his daughter Maria on her marriage to the Duke of Edinburgh. This tiara and the brooch below were inherited by her daughter, Queen Marie of Romania.

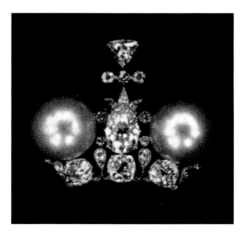

A brooch belonging to the Duchess of Edinburgh, in the form of an imperial Russian crown, set with two large Oriental pearls, one white and one grey.

OVERLEAF: The marriage of Princess Marie of Edinburgh and Prince Ferdinand of Romania celebrated in the *Illustrated London News* of 14 January 1893.

THE MARRIAGE OF PRIN

Photo of the Princess by Heath,

MARIE OF EDINBURGH.

Prince by Mandy, Bucharest,

Next, Victoria Melita married Ernst Ludwig, Grand Duke of Hesse, at Coburg on 19 April 1894. One of Ernst Ludwig's sisters had married Victoria Melita's uncle, Grand Duke Sergei, and become Grand Duchess Elizabeth of Russia, and another sister was Princess Alix, whose engagement to the future Tsar Nicholas II was officially announced at this event. When Nicholas and Alix's wedding took place a few months later, Victoria Melita was pregnant and could not accompany her husband.

Victoria Melita took great delight in the company of her sister Marie, whom she and the rest of the family called 'Missy', while her own nickname was 'Ducky'. In 1895 they spent a holiday together on the Isle of Wight, Missy accompanied by her infant son Carol (born in October 1893) and daughter Elizabeth (born in October 1894), and Ducky with her baby Elizabeth, known as Ella, who was born in March.

The two sisters were soon reunited in May 1896 for the coronation of the Tsar and Tsarina. We can see them in a photograph taken at the Grand Ball [*opposite*], when they are accompanied not only by their spouses but by their parents and brother Alfred. Missy and Ducky's mother, Maria, Duchess of Edinburgh and Saxe-Coburg-Gotha, is wearing an opulent court dress with the jewelry given to her for own wedding by her father, Tsar Alexander II – the splendid *parure* of rubies and diamonds and large *tiare russe* also set with diamonds [78–81]. From descriptions of the ball it is clear that all the grand duchesses and royal guests displayed the most beautiful jewelry from their collections. Grand Duchess Xenia (the Tsar's sister) was swathed in emeralds, while Grand Duchess Vladimir (his aunt) was bedecked with precious ropes of pearls and a velvet *kokoshnik* on which her necklace of drop pearls encircled by diamonds had been mounted [107]. For Marie and Victoria Melita, the coronation was an opportunity to experience the splendour of the Russian court – completely unknown to them before they were married – and to show off their elegant dresses and exceptional jewelry.

Despite their period of engagement, Victoria Melita and Ernst Ludwig had not been able to get to know each another well, and it was only after their marriage that the differences in their characters began to emerge. The young Grand Duchess soon began to find life in the little grand duchy of Hesse dull and restrictive, and she was uncomfortable with the official duties that accompanied her status. It is said that she would frequently cause great embarrassment at official receptions by only talking to people whom she liked, which made her husband extremely uncomfortable. Furthermore, as she was an experienced horsewoman, Victoria Melita loved to spend a great deal of time riding in the country, rather than attending to her official duties. Inevitably, Tsarina Alexandra formed an ever lower opinion of her sister-in-law.

The Duke and Duchess of Edinburgh and Saxe-Coburg-Gotha with two
of their daughters and their son at a ball celebrating the coronation of
Tsar Nicholas II in May 1896. Seated are the Duchess and, on the left,
her daughter Marie, Crown Princess of Romania. Standing, from left to right,
are a page, then Crown Prince Ferdinand of Romania (husband of Marie),
Grand Duke Ernst Ludwig of Hesse (husband of Victoria Melita), another
page, the Duke, Victoria Melita, Grand Duchess of Hesse, Prince Alfred,
and another page. The Duchess is wearing her ruby *parure* [78–79]
and *tiare russe* [81].

Grand Duke Sergei
and Grand Duchess Elizabeth

Grand Duke Sergei Alexandrovich (1857–1905) married Princess Elizabeth of Hesse, sister of the future Empress Alexandra Feodorovna, in 1884. The couple had no children, but were to become very close to those of Sergei's brother, Grand Duke Paul (see pp. 132–33). It was at their estate of Ilinskoye near Moscow in 1891 that Paul's young wife died after giving birth to her second child. Paul later met and fell in love with Olga von Pistohlkors, the wife of an army officer; their relationship was not approved of, and Paul's children by his wife, Grand Duchess Maria Pavlovna and Grand Duke Dmitri Pavlovich, lived with their uncle and aunt at Ilinskoye. When Paul and Olga married in 1902 (see p. 133) he was banished from Russia, and Sergei became the legal guardian of the two children, He treated them with great love and attention – to the degree that, Maria later recalled, Grand Duchess Elizabeth (known in the family as Ella) – showed signs of jealousy. Furthermore, as a devout Catholic, she could never forgive her brother-in-law Paul for coveting another man's wife and breaking the bond of matrimony.

Grand Duke Sergei served as Governor General of Moscow, and in that role after the coronation of Nicholas II and Alexandra in 1896 he was involved in events surrounding the disastrous panic and ensuing deaths in the Khodynka Meadow (see pp. 36–42). The general organization of the coronation had been in the hands of Count Vorontsov-Dashkov, the Minister of the Court, while Sergei was responsible for the security of the city. The Dowager Empress could not understand why the police had not been deployed to control the ever-growing crowd, and, supported by most of the family, she blamed Sergei for not having been equal to the task. In his attempt to avoid any personal responsibility for the disaster, he placed the blame on Count Vorontsov-Dashkov, and he also avoided visiting the scene of the disaster. As we have seen, he was instrumental in persuading Nicholas II not to cancel the ball at the French Embassy, for fear of offending the representative of Russia's only European ally. When the Tsar's sister, Grand Duchess Xenia, tried to express her doubts to Grand Duchess Elizabeth, she received the reply: 'Thanks be to God, Sergei had nothing to do with all this!' When the Tsar proposed to set up an inquiry, Sergei threatened to resign his governorship.

Grand Duke Sergei's inability to maintain order as Governor General of Moscow was to prove fatal to him a few years later, in 1905, when as we have seen revolutionary feelings were boiling up in Russia (see p. 55).

His views were extreme, and he resisted all attempts at mediation: it was his firm conviction that any revolutionary ferment must be snuffed out at once. Seeing that a softer line was being taken to the demands of the workers, he resigned as Governor – but still kept command of the city's military forces. Together with his wife Elizabeth and his niece and nephew, he moved from the Governor's Palace to a building not far away. He still returned regularly to his former office to collect documents and personal possessions, however, and on 17 February, as the carriage was passing through Senate Square, the anarchist Ivan Platonovich Kalyayev threw a bomb which destroyed the carriage and killed Sergei.

When Grand Duke Paul, who had obtained permission to return to Russia to attend his brother's funeral, met his sister-in-law, he was made aware of Elizabeth's continuing resentment over his marriage to Olga. Paul was the only brother to attend the funeral, since in the troubled year of 1905 the imperial family had been warned to avoid appearing at public events for fear of attacks. The ceremony was preceded, in accordance with imperial etiquette, by the lying in state in the church of St Alexis in the Chudov Monastery, within the walls of the Kremlin. The body of Grand Duke Sergei was dressed in the uniform of the regiment of the Grenadiers of Kiev; in his gloved hands, resting on his chest, was an icon of St Nicholas; his disfigured face was covered by a veil of fine Brussels lace. Then, after the long official funeral ceremony, the coffin was carried by grand dukes and generals to the church of St Andrew in the monastery, where the coffin was buried. Afterwards, the crowd gathered at the site of his assassination: there a small enclosure had been created within which, amid a mound of crowns, there was an iron cross, surmounted by a lamp kept lit night and day.

Elizabeth had asked Maria and Dmitri for forgiveness for the involuntary feelings of jealousy she had felt towards them when her husband was still alive. She visited the assassin in prison and forgave him (he was hanged three months later). Her attitude to Grand Duke Paul remained inflexible, however; she was now his children's guardian, and she would not consent to their seeing more of their father.

After her husband's death the Grand Duchess sold much of her jewelry to fund an organization to assist the destitute of the city of Moscow, administered by the Convent of Martha and Mary, of which she became abbess, having taken religious vows. Other pieces were returned to the Imperial Treasury, or given to the Hesse family, and she gave her magnificent emerald and diamond *kokoshnik* and *parure* to her niece, Maria Pavlovna the Younger (who later sold them to King Alexander of Serbia) [91, 274, 275, 277–79]. After war broke out, she dedicated herself to caring for the wounded, transported to her estate at Ilinskoye.

Before she married, in 1884, the Grand Duchess Sergius was Princess Elizabeth Alexandra Louise Alice of Hesse, the second daughter of the late Grand Duke of Hesse and of our own beloved Princess Alice. She was born in 1864.

GRAND DUKE SERGIUS UNCLE OF THE CZAR
Late Governor of Moscow   Feared Throughout Russia.

The Grand Duke Sergius Alexandrowitch is the third uncle of the Czar and the brother of Marie Duchess of Saxe-Coburg-Gotha. He was born in 1857 and earned an unenviable reputation as Governor of Moscow, a position of which he was relieved only the other day.

ABOVE: Grand Duke Sergei and Grand
Duchess Elizabeth in the early 20th century.

RIGHT: Grand Duke Sergei and Grand
Duchess Elizabeth with members
of his staff. At her neck she wears
a brooch in the form of an imperial
crown set with diamonds, one of those
commissioned by Nicholas II from Fabergé
for the Russian grand duchesses to
commemorate his coronation.

ABOVE: Grand Duchess Elizabeth's large *devant de corsage* in emeralds and diamonds. This extraordinary jewel, designed as a triple cascade of pear-shaped cabochon emeralds, appeared in November 1911 in the sale of the treasures of the Turkish Sultan Abdul Hamid II at the Galerie Georges Petit in Paris. It appears worn by the Grand Duchess in the photograph opposite. When after the assassination of her husband in 1905 the Grand Duchess sold many of her jewels to fund a charitable convent, an extraordinary piece such as this *devant de corsage* was so valuable and recognizable that it was not wise to sell it in Russia: for that reason, one can only assume, it ended up on the international market and was acquired by the Sultan.

OPPOSITE: Grand Duchess Elizabeth with a lady-in-waiting in 1897. She is wearing the *devant de corsage* seen above, and also an emerald and diamond necklace. On her fabric *kokoshnik*, elements from her emerald and diamond *kokoshnik* designed by the court jeweller Bolin are mounted in alternation with diamond leaves dating from the time of Catherine the Great, from the Imperial Treasury. She later gave the emerald and diamond necklace and *kokoshnik* to her niece, Grand Duchess Maria Pavlovna the Younger, from whom they were eventually bought for Queen Marie of Serbia by her husband, King Alexander [274, 275, 277–79].

OPPOSITE: The spot in Senate Square in the Kremlin in Moscow where Grand Duke Sergei was assassinated in February 1905. It is fenced off, and marked with an iron cross.

ABOVE LEFT: Grand Duchess Elizabeth, in mourning for her husband, Grand Duke Sergei, with Maria Pavlovna the Younger and Dmitri Pavlovich – children of her brother-in-law, Grand Duke Paul, of whom she had become guardian after her husband's death.

ABOVE RIGHT: Grand Duchess Elizabeth as abbess of the Convent of Mary and Martha in Moscow.

Grand Duke Vladimir and his Family

Grand Duke Vladimir Alexandrovich (1847–1909) was the second son of Alexander II, and the brother of Alexander III. In 1871 he met Princess Marie of Mecklenburg-Schwerin, a descendant of Tsar Paul I, who was to become his wife. Marie was just seventeen, and betrothed to a German prince, but on meeting Vladimir she broke off that engagement. An obstacle to the marriage of Vladimir and Marie was her refusal to convert to the Russian Orthodox faith, contradicting a strict tradition that had applied to generations of Romanov spouses. Negotiations continued between the two courts for three years, until, in the spring of 1874, Alexander II consented to the union. (The decision angered many of the princesses who had had no choice but to convert in order to marry grand dukes of the imperial family.) As Grand Duchess, Marie took the name of Maria Pavlovna.

The 'court' of Grand Duke and Grand Duchess Vladimir was rivalled in splendour only by that of the Tsar himself. Their residence, on the Palace Embankment in St Petersburg not far from the Winter Palace, was built specially for them: designed by a team of architects including Alexander Rezanov and Andrei Huhn, and unusual in being in Florentine Renaissance style, it was completed on 10 August 1874, and the couple took up residence a week later. The first floor was the realm of the Grand Duchess.

Grand Duke Vladimir, who was a Councillor of State, member of the Council of Ministers and field commander of the guard for the military district of St Petersburg, was also a lover of literature and the arts, and presided over the Imperial Academy of Arts. Very soon, the salons of the Vladimir Palace became the centre of cultural and social life in St Petersburg – the setting for prestigious concerts and sumptuous masquerade balls, for encounters between politicians and diplomats, and for gatherings of artists, musicians and intellectuals from all parts of Europe.

OPPOSITE: Maria Pavlovna, Grand Duchess Vladimir, in the Vladimir Palace, wearing court dress bordered with Russian sable. Her jewels include the splendid *kokoshnik* with its diamond-set interlaced circles and drop pearls made for her by the court jeweller Bolin at the time of her wedding in 1874 [99] and a magnificent pearl and diamond necklace similar to one in the Imperial Treasury [106].

OVERLEAF: The Vladimir Palace, on the Palace Embankment in St Petersburg, completed for Grand Duke Vladimir and his Grand Duchess in the year of their marriage, 1874.

In 1875 their first son was born, Grand Duke Alexander, who lived for only two years. He was followed in 1876 by Grand Duke Cyril, and a year later by Grand Duke Boris; Grand Duke Andrei was born in 1879, and finally, in 1883, Grand Duchess Elena.

Blessed with a strong personality and great charm, Grand Duchess Maria Pavlovna (known in the family as 'Miechen') was very well aware of her role and of the need to exercise it with elegant refinement. On her marriage, she received a splendid *parure* from Alexander II [100–101]. It included an emerald necklace of which the centrepiece was a hexagonal emerald weighing 100 carats, set in a double border of diamonds in traditional Russian style; nine other similarly set stones alternated with circular motifs of diamonds, and a large pear-shaped cabochon emerald was suspended from each of the emerald elements. All the sections were detachable, so the necklace could be worn in different ways. Also in the *parure* was a brooch with a rectangular-cut emerald of 107.72 carats said to have belonged to Catherine the Great, surrounded by a double row of diamonds in the same design as the necklace settings, from which a pear-shaped cabochon emerald also surrounded with diamonds was suspended [100, 101].

One of Maria Pavlovna's favourite pieces of jewelry was a tiara in the shape of a *kokoshnik*, made up of fifteen interlaced circles, which had been created by the court jeweller Bolin especially for her wedding [99]. Drop pearls, unique for their perfect shape and even colour, were suspended from openings in the circles. The *kokoshnik* could be removed from the structure that supported it, and be worn with or without its drop pearls.

The strings of pearls worn by the Grand Duchess were legendary: in 1896, for the coronation of her nephew, Nicholas II, her neck and shoulders were memorably swathed in pearls [107].

continued on page 108...

OPPOSITE, ABOVE: The spectacular *kokoshnik* made for Grand Duchess Vladimir by the court jeweller Bolin at the time of her wedding in 1874. It has a design of interlaced circles set with diamonds, and perfect drop pearls hang from a ribbon motif that winds through the top of the circles. (The *kokoshnik* was inherited by the Grand Duchess's daughter Elena. She sold it to Queen Mary, consort of George V, King of Great Britain, and today it is one of the pieces of jewelry worn most frequently by Queen Elizabeth II.)

OPPOSITE, BELOW: A brooch with a large natural pearl as its centrepiece, flanked by two cushion-cut diamonds and set within an oval border of old-cut diamonds from which three detachable pendants, each one set with a pear-shaped diamond, are suspended. This jewel too survived the Revolution, and was subsequently sold from the Grand Duchess's collection.

ABOVE: The Grand Duchess wearing elements of the *parure* with the boyar costume she wore for the Bal des Costumes Russes in 1903 [*cf.* 46–47, 66–67]. Her headdress incorporates the necklace seen opposite. Pinned to her costume is the brooch, with a rectangular-cut emerald weighing 107.72 carats in a double row of old-cut diamonds, from which a pear-shaped cabochon emerald also encircled by diamonds was suspended.

OPPOSITE: The emerald and diamond necklace from the *parure* that Grand Duchess Vladimir received from Tsar Alexander II as a wedding present in 1874, with a central hexagonal stone weighing 100 carats.

LEFT: The emerald from the Grand Duchess's brooch as recut in pear shape by Cartier in 1954 (to remove a natural inclusion in the stone), reducing it to 75.63 carats. Grand Duke Boris had sold the brooch to Cartier in 1927, and Ralph Esmerian had advised its recutting; the emerald became the pendant in an emerald necklace bought from the Payne Whitney family and sold to John D. Rockefeller Jr, who eventually sold it at Sotheby's in 1971. Boris had sold the necklace to Cartier earlier, and it had crossed the Atlantic, to be broken up and its emeralds incorporated, sometimes recut, into a variety of jewels for wealthy international clients (including, in the United States, Edith Rockefeller McCormick and Barbara Hutton).

Formal portrait photographs of Grand Duke Vladimir and Grand Duchess
Maria Pavlovna in their youth. The Grand Duchess is wearing a tiara with
the cushion-cut sapphire and diamonds which were later used for the
kokoshnik that Cartier made for her in 1909 [114].

Grand Duke Vladimir and Grand Duchess Maria Pavlovna photographed in 1884 with their children – from left ro right Boris, Elena, Cyril and Andrei.

ABOVE: A Star of the Order of St Alexander Nevsky, set with diamonds, dating from the end of the 19th century. The initials 'S.S.' in the centre are encircled with the motto of the Order, 'For Labour and Fatherland', in Cyrillic letters on a background of red enamel and surmounted by the imperial crown in diamonds. The Grand Duchess would have worn the star on formal occasions [*cf.* 27].

OPPOSITE: Grand Duchess Vladimir and Zenaida Dmitrievna, Comtesse de Beauharnais, wife of the 5th Duke of Leuchtenberg (see pp. 160–65), dressed for a costume ball in the late 1880s.

OPPOSITE: A necklace formed of a string of pearls interspersed with fifteen diamond motifs from which hang pearl drops encircled by old-cut diamonds, mounted in gold and silver. This splendid example of mid-19th century goldsmith's art belonged to the Imperial Treasury.

ABOVE: Grand Duchess Vladimir – on the right – and her sister-in-law, Grand Duchess of Mecklenburg-Schwerin (Grand Duchess Anastasia Mikhailovna), at the Coronation Ball in 1896. She wears on a velvet *kokoshnik* her pearl necklace with pendant diamonds and drop pearls [*see also* 95], very similar to the one from the Imperial Treasury seen opposite, and her remarkable strings of pearls.

On her frequent visits to Paris, Maria Pavlovna became fascinated by Chaumet's magnificent creations. In 1899, to celebrate her silver wedding, she acquired a splendid head ornament, its central motif like a fountain with pear-shaped diamonds which trembled with every movement of the head, flanked by elements also designed as sprays of water, the many pear-shaped diamonds adding to the sensational dynamic effect [111]. The Grand Duchess remained a client of Chaumet until 1914. (To mark their wedding anniversaries the Grand Duke and Grand Duchess also commissioned cufflinks from Fabergé [294–95].)

In 1900 Grand Duchess Vladimir met Pierre Cartier. She was a great connoisseur of gemstones, and in him she found a kindred spirit. Their

Grand Duke and Grand Duchess Vladimir photographed on the occasion of their silver wedding anniversary in 1899 with their children – from left to right, Grand Duke Andrei, Grand Duchess Elena, Grand Duke Cyril and Grand Duke Boris.

On his coronation in 1896 Nicholas II gave Grand
Duke Vladimir – his uncle – and the Grand Duchess
this box, made by Michael Perkhin for Fabergé.
The cover is decorated with the Tsar's monogram
in diamonds on a lozenge of white opaque enamel
bordered with diamonds, set against a background
of translucent green enamel edged with laurel
leaves and ribbons. Inside it, on a card with
Tsarina Alexandra's monogram, is a handwritten
note from Nicholas II which reads: 'Alix
and I ask you to accept this small present
as a souvenir of this day! Nicky'.

LEFT: Grand Duchess Vladimir photographed in Paris by Otto (Otto Wegener) at the turn of the century, wearing a tiara of aigrette form. The photograph appeared in the magazine *The King* on 20 February 1904.

OPPOSITE: The waterfall tiara created by Chaumet in 1899. Elements fashioned to imitate sprays of water, set with diamonds, support pear-shaped diamonds which tremble with every movement. The total weight of diamonds in this spectacular piece was more than 75 carats. It may be assumed that the tiara was a present from the Grand Duke to the Grand Duchess to celebrate their silver wedding in that year.

collaboration was to see the creation of sensational jewels for her collection. In that year she ordered a choker formed of six strands of pearls with two double-headed imperial Russian eagles [*above and opposite*]. The eagles were completely covered with diamonds, and their tails were articulated so that they rested on her neck. In 1908 she had the historic octagonal Beauharnais ruby reset as the centrepiece of a *kokoshnik* made from diamonds and decorated with cabochon rubies. In 1909 – the year of her husband's death – Cartier created one of the most spectacular pieces in her collection, a *kokoshnik* of sapphires and diamonds [114–15], based on an existing diamond setting from the stock of his Parisian shop in the Rue de la Paix. Maria Pavlovna herself provided a cushion-cut sapphire weighing 137.20 carats (which had previously been the centrepiece of a tiara with a typical Russian setting of a double row of diamonds [102]). It retained its original mount and became the central motif of the *kokoshnik,* where it was joined by another six sapphires weighing a total of 102.16 carats. All the motifs in diamonds and sapphires were detachable and could be worn as brooches. Cartier travelled specially to St Petersburg to deliver this exquisite piece of jewelry in person. In 1910, the Grand Duchess decided to have a *devant de corsage* made which could be worn as a *parure* with the *kokoshnik* [114–15].

She again provided various pieces of jewelry to be disassembled and the stones re-used (a list is preserved in the Cartier archives of all the jewelry that the Grand Duchess supplied for the purpose); an oval sapphire weighing 162 carats formed the centrepiece. Her relationship with Cartier continued until the eve of the Great War: in 1913 she ordered a pendant decorated with six briolette diamonds weighing more than 42 carats, and purchased a pear-shaped diamond of almost 40 carats.

OPPOSITE, ABOVE: A *collier de chien* made by Cartier in 1900 for the
Grand Duchess, with six strings of pearls and two large imperial eagles
set with diamonds.

ABOVE: A photograph taken by Otto in Paris of the Grand Duchess wearing
the *collier de chien*. It is shown here in a frame by Fabergé designed to be
displayed on a dressing table, which originally held a mirror. This has
translucent red guilloché enamel overlaid with imperial Russian eagles;
at the top, a disc of opaque white enamel contains the Grand Duchess's
monogram surmounted by the imperial crown, all set in diamonds.

OPPOSITE, BELOW: A diamond and sapphire brooch with an oval sapphire in
the centre and a double border of cushion-cut diamonds, and a pair of earrings
en suite. The brooch bears the initials of its creator, Sophia Schwan, who
worked for Bolin in St Petersburg; it was probably made in Bolin's workshop
at the start of the 20th century. (Brooch and earrings were eventually inherited
by Grand Duchess Elena.)

OPPOSITE, ABOVE: The *kokoshnik* made by Cartier in 1909. In the centre is a cushion-cut sapphire weighing 137.20 carats supplied by the Grand Duchess, in its original Russian setting in a double row of diamonds; it is accompanied by six more cabochon sapphires, set in diamond borders.

OPPOSITE, BELOW: The *devant de corsage* commissioned from Cartier in 1910 to accompany the *kokoshnik* with at its centre an oval sapphire weighing 162 carats.

ABOVE: Grand Duchess Vladimir wearing her fabulous sapphire *parure*, painted by Boris Kustodiev in 1913.

The first of the four Vladimirovich children to marry was Grand Duchess Elena, who became the wife of Prince Nicholas of Greece and Denmark in 1902. For a wedding present, her mother ordered a diamond *kokoshnik* from Cartier with a classic vine motif and pear-shaped diamonds [*above and opposite*]. Elena's cousin, Nicholas II, gave her a traditional diamond *tiare russe* of the type given to all grand duchesses, which could also be worn as a necklace.

ABOVE: The diamond *kokoshnik* commissioned from Cartier by Grand Duchess Vladimir as a present for her daughter, Grand Duchess Elena, on her marriage to Prince Nicholas of Greece and Denmark in 1902.

OPPOSITE: Grand Duchess Elena, wearing the *kokoshnik* given to her by her mother (seen above) and a large bow-shaped *devant de corsage* in diamonds. She later gave the *devant de corsage* to her daughter Marina, who married the Duke of Kent, son of George V, King of Great Britain.

ABOVE: Grand Duchess Elena and Prince Nicholas of Greece and Denmark on their wedding day in 1902. She is wearing the jewelry and mantle traditionally worn by Russian grand duchesses on their wedding day [51, 53, 249–51].

OPPOSITE: A cigarette case commemorating the wedding of Grand Duchess Elena and Prince Nicholas, made by Michael Perkhin for Fabergé in 1902. The case is decorated with alternate stripes of opaque green and mauve enamel. On the front are applied miniatures of the royal couple, by Zengraf, flanking Cupid's arrow below a ribbon-tied festoon.

THIS PAGE: Diamond and pearl jewelry remounted by Cartier for Princess Elena of Greece and Denmark using stones from the Romanov collection. In the jewel bottom right, the drop pearl retains its original 1890 setting.

OPPOSITE, INSET: A commemorative brooch for the wedding of Grand Duchess Elena and Prince Nicholas of Greece and Denmark designed by Friedrich Koechli in 1902. The heart-shaped frame with diamonds of various different cuts, surmounted by the royal crown, contains portrait miniatures of the couple mounted in borders of rose diamonds.

OPPOSITE, MAIN PICTURE: Princess Elena photographed in 1909 with her three daughters: Olga, who is leaning on her mother's shoulder, Elizabeth, to the right, and Marina.

ABOVE: Grand Duke Cyril Vladimirovich, Grand Duchess Victoria Melita, and their little daughter Maria, photographed in Coburg before their return to Russia.

LEFT: Grand Duchess Victoria Melita in 1909 with her daughter Maria and her baby daughter Kyra in her arms. The Grand Duchess is wearing an imposing *parure* consisting of a necklace, *devant de corsage* and tiara in diamonds and sapphires – probably a gift from her mother-in-law, Grand Duchess Vladimir.

The eldest of the Vladimirovich children, Grand Duke Cyril, had fallen in love with Victoria Melita, who was his cousin and the cousin of Nicholas II. She was, however, already married to Tsarina Alexandra's brother, Grand Duke Ernst Ludwig of Hesse (see p. 84). This threw the family into considerable turmoil. Eventually Victoria Melita divorced her husband, and in the autumn of 1905 Grand Duke Cyril decided to formalize their relationship. On 8 October Father Smirnov arrived at the place they had chosen for their wedding – the home of Count Adlerberg near Tegernsee, not far from Munich – and conducted the service. A few days later, the Grand Duke returned to St Petersburg and told the news to his father, who seemed reasonably content. He intended to visit the Tsar the following day. Things did not work out as he expected. In his memoirs, Cyril records that on the evening of his arrival in St Petersburg he dined with his father and guests and was playing bridge when a valet announced the arrival of Count Friederickes, a Minister of the Court. Friederickes had been sent to tell Cyril Vladimirovich that he was to leave Russia within 48 hours, that he was deprived of all his honours, and that he was now excluded from the army and the navy. The Grand Duke wrote:

> The next day, my father was absolutely outraged at the conduct of his nephew the Tsar, and when he realized that the Emperor would not relent, he resigned his commission as commander-in-chief of the military district of St Petersburg. This sudden change in my situation, however, did not cast a shadow over my life or that of my wife. For the next three years we travelled through Europe. In January 1907, Ducky converted to the Russian Orthodox faith, and a month later, on 2 February, in the Villa Edinburgh in Coburg, she gave birth to our daughter Maria. In the autumn of 1908, while we were in Paris, we received news of the death of my uncle, Grand Duke Alexei Alexandrovich. I was given permission to return to Russia for the funeral; during the ceremonies I was able to wear my uniform, as a mark of the imperial favour obtained for me by my brother.
>
> At the start of 1909 my father became gravely ill, and he died on 13 February of that year. Boris had been actively campaigning for my complete rehabilitation in Russia, and a few days before the death of my father, I received a short telegram from my mother who wrote: 'Your wife is a Grand Duchess', and I still guard this jealously today. These few words in fact meant that everything could now revert to normal and that we would soon go back to Russia. I returned for my father's funeral, and the Emperor and Empress were very courteous when we met.

RIGHT: The sapphire and diamond necklace by Cartier given to Grand Duchess Victoria Melita by her husband Cyril for Christmas in 1911.

BELOW: The Grand Duchess wearing the necklace.

On 9 May 1909, in our home in Paris on the Avenue Henry Martin, our second child, Kyra, was born. I had just been appointed second-in-command of the cruiser *Oleg*. On 18 April 1910, I was promoted to the rank of captain, and in the following month my family and I were finally able to begin our life in Russia.

Photographs taken after Victoria Melita's acceptance as Grand Duchess show her wearing a magnificent sapphire and diamond *parure* [122], probably made in Russia in the second half of the 19th century, which may well have been a gift from her mother-in-law. The diamond tiara with a Greek key design that Victoria usually wore sewn onto a fabric *kokoshnik* also dates from this period. In St Petersburg, on Christmas Day 1911, Grand Duke Cyril presented his wife with a sapphire and diamond necklace by Cartier, made of a series of oval links in platinum and diamonds [*opposite*]; from the centrepiece – a cabochon sapphire weighing 35 carats encircled by diamonds – a line of oval links identical to the chain above supported an oval cabochon sapphire weighing 311.33 carats.

Of the other Vladimirovich children, Grand Duke Boris took an active part in the social life of St Petersburg, and conducted numerous affairs until he asked the Tsar for the hand of his daughter, Grand Duchess Olga. The Tsarina took great offence at this, and was so outraged that she forbade any further discussion of the matter.

The youngest son, Andrei, fell deeply in love with Mathilde Kschessinska (see below, pp. 169–72), but Nicholas II denied him permission to marry the ballet dancer who had been his own mistress. However, the relationship between Andrei and the ballerina continued and in 1903 their son Vladimir – always known in the family as Vova – was born. The bond between the two proved to be very strong: they managed to escape from Russia, and subsequently married in France and settled in Paris. There Mathilde proved herself to be very courageous and full of spirit: by opening a ballet school she was able to keep the family, and she remained Andrei's faithful companion for the rest of his life, proving herself superior to all the spiteful gossip that had circulated about her in St Petersburg.

In 1917 strikes and demonstrations were becoming more frequent in St Petersburg – or rather Petrograd, as it had been renamed in 1914 – where, as the British Ambassador, Sir George Buchanan, wrote in his memoirs, 'Robberies and murders have become a daily occurrence, and at night people are attacked on the streets and stripped of their clothes and any objects of value, and not a night goes by without one hearing the constant sound of shooting.' Grand Duchess Vladimir left for Kislovodsk in the Caucasus – where her son Andrei and Mathilde Kschessinska had already

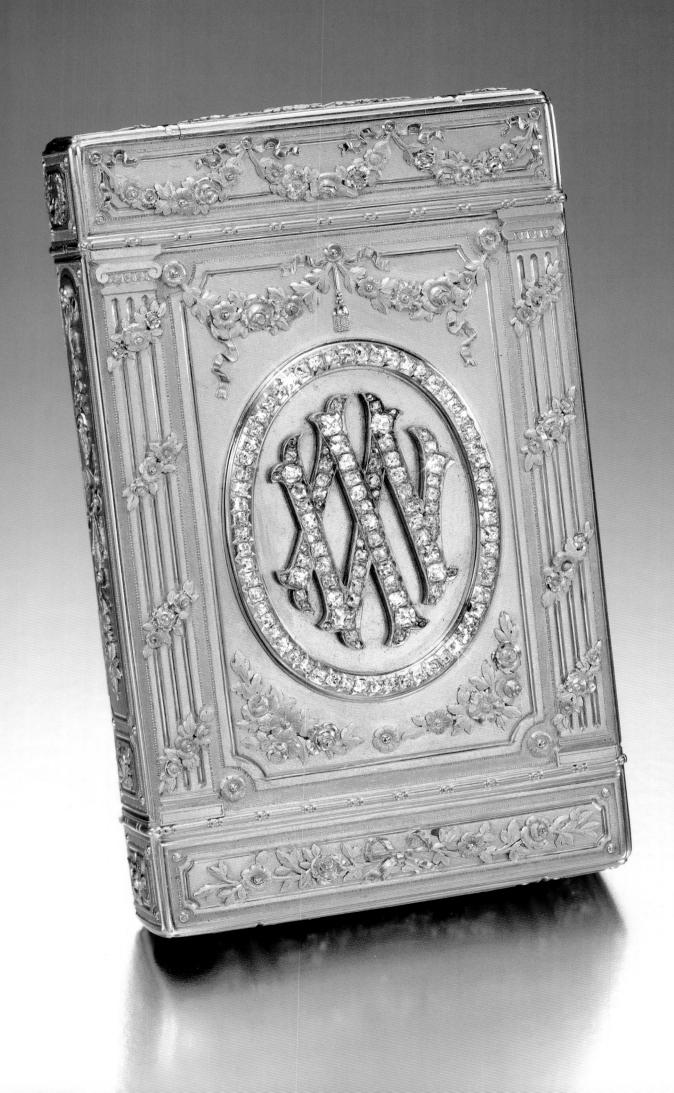

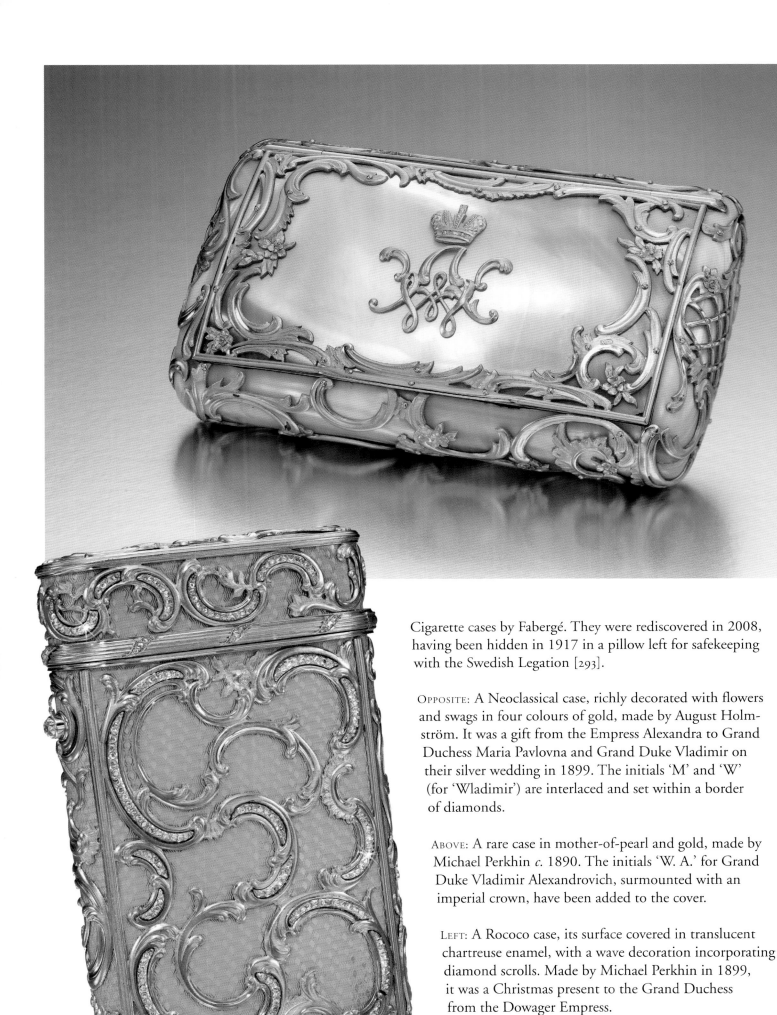

Cigarette cases by Fabergé. They were rediscovered in 2008, having been hidden in 1917 in a pillow left for safekeeping with the Swedish Legation [293].

OPPOSITE: A Neoclassical case, richly decorated with flowers and swags in four colours of gold, made by August Holmström. It was a gift from the Empress Alexandra to Grand Duchess Maria Pavlovna and Grand Duke Vladimir on their silver wedding in 1899. The initials 'M' and 'W' (for 'Wladimir') are interlaced and set within a border of diamonds.

ABOVE: A rare case in mother-of-pearl and gold, made by Michael Perkhin c. 1890. The initials 'W. A.' for Grand Duke Vladimir Alexandrovich, surmounted with an imperial crown, have been added to the cover.

LEFT: A Rococo case, its surface covered in translucent chartreuse enamel, with a wave decoration incorporating diamond scrolls. Made by Michael Perkhin in 1899, it was a Christmas present to the Grand Duchess from the Dowager Empress.

rented a villa – and called on a faithful friend, the Hon. Albert Henry Stopford, to take care of her jewelry. (Thanks to influential friends such as the Marchioness of Ripon and Prince Felix Yusupov, Stopford had established close relationships with members of the Russian imperial family, and made regular visits to St Petersburg.) He went to check that the Vladimir Palace had not yet been sacked, and travelled to Kislovodsk to report, where he found the Grand Duchess being held under house arrest by the city's Red Committee after one day in prison.

Stopford returned to the capital and enlisted the help of Grand Duke Boris – who had himself been held under arrest in his house at Tsarskoe Selo – to save Maria Pavlovna's jewelry before the authorities seized the palace. The main entrances overlooking the Neva were too exposed, they decided. A small side entrance at the east led to the kitchens, and from there, the Grand Duchess had explained, a secret passage led directly to her Moorish-style boudoir on the first floor, from which a hidden door led via narrow passageways to the place where the strongbox was concealed, between the wardrobe and the dressing room. In the middle of the night pford, dressed as a workman, left his little hotel and reached the palace. Following Maria Pavlovna's instructions, with the assistance of a faithful family servant he found the strongbox. He removed the tiaras from their supports and took the pieces of jewelry from their boxes, wrapped everything carefully in newspaper and placed it in two old Gladstone bags, together with money which he had also rescued. That, he thought, was the easiest part of the undertaking. He now had to walk with the bags through streets full of soldiers and criminal gangs. His hotel room had been searched, and might be again. We may assume that he left the two bags in safety in the chancellery of the British Embassy, where he kept his own documents.

Stopford went back to Tsarskoe Selo to reassure Grand Duke Boris that everything had gone well, and learned that the imperial family were likely to be transported to Siberia, which until then had been a closely guarded secret. The next day, 28 July, he hid the money in his boots and travelled by train to the Caucasus to see Maria Pavlovna. On 5 August he returned to Petrograd with the intention of taking the Grand Duchess's jewels out of Russia. A diplomatic bag could easily be checked. But through its commander, a friend, he knew that the Russian Armoured Car Division, a Special Unit of the Royal Navy which had been active in Russia since 1905, was to be evacuated. Their plan was for an initial company of soldiers to depart from Archangel in the third week of August. Among the first to leave was a young Englishman called John Stopford. It is unclear whether Albert Stopford already knew of the young man, and also unclear how the papers were arranged, but the departure of the two Stopfords coincided. Albert left Petrograd on 26 September and went via Sweden to London with the precious goods. Before leaving, however, he had been able to congratulate himself when he learnt that a Revolutionary Committee of soldiers and workers had invaded the Vladimir Palace and searched in vain for the jewelry. (In 1919 Countess Elizabeth Shuvalov, a friend of Grand Duchess Vladimir, persuaded Stopford to allow his memoirs to be published, and they appeared anonymously under the title of *The Russian Diary of an Englishman (1915–1917).*)

It is highly likely that the splendid collection of Fabergé cigarette cases and a large collection of cufflinks belonging to Grand Duke Vladimir were also concealed at this time. Almost a year after Stopford's rescue mission, Professor Richard Alexandrovich Bergholz, head of the Union of Russian Artists, appeared at the Swedish Legation with two pillows bearing seals and an inscription in French, 'Appartient à S.A.I. la Gr. Duchesse Vladimir' (Belonging to Her Imperial Highness Grand Duchess Vladimir), which unknown to all were filled with these precious things. Professor Bergholz would certainly have known Maria Pavlovna, since she had taken over her husband's position as President of the Imperial Academy of Art after his death in 1909. It is impossible to know whether Stopford had prepared the pillows with the help of the same faithful servant who had then hidden them in a safe place, or whether the servant had given them directly to Bergholz, who then concealed them for almost a year. Their delivery coincided with the severance of diplomatic relations between Russia and Sweden, and the Swedish officials took not only their diplomatic paperwork but the pillows to Stockholm at the end of 1918. (The pillows and their contents were finally rediscovered in 2008: see pp. 289–93.)

The Grand Duchess remained in Kislovodsk until January 1918. She had been greatly distressed by her period of arrest and by her house being invaded by wandering revolutionary soldiers. But now the Red Army arrived in the Caucasus, and her presence became problematic. The last of the Romanovs to depart, she set out from Kislovodsk in a special train, under the protection of a leader of the White Russian Army, for the port of Novorossiysk. She lived in the train for six weeks before the *Semiranisa*, an Italian liner sailing directly to Venice, docked, and the Grand Duchess was able to embark, together with her son Andrei accompanied by Mathilde Kschessinska and their son Vova, and her son Boris with his companion Zina Rachevsky (they would marry in 1919).

Grand Duke Paul and his Family

Grand Duke Paul Alexandrovich (1860–1919) was the youngest son of Alexander II and Maria Alexandrovna. He was a general in the cavalry, adjutant general to his brother, the Emperor Alexander III, and a Knight of the Order of St Andrew.

In 1889 he married Princess Alexandra of Greece, who became Grand Duchess Alexandra Georgievna; she was the daughter of King George I and Grand Duchess Olga Constantinovna of Russia. In 1890 their first daughter, Maria Pavlovna, was born (she was to be known in the family as 'Maria Pavlovna the Younger' to distinguish her from Grand Duchess Vladimir). In 1891, during a visit to Ilinskoye, an estate not far from Moscow belonging to Paul's brother, Grand Duke Sergei Alexandrovich, and his wife Grand Duchess Elizabeth Feodorovna (on Sergei and Elizabeth see above, pp. 86–93), Alexandra, who was seven months pregnant with her second child, suddenly became ill and fell into a coma for six days. Paul never moved from the side of his young consort – Alexandra was only twenty-one years old – but the Grand Duchess died after giving birth to their son, Grand Duke Dmitri Pavlovich.

Paul was inconsolable, but found comfort in the loving care of his brother and sister-in-law. After a period of deep mourning, he returned to life with his regiment and to his service duties, thus allowing the social life of St Petersburg to return to normal. As his sister-in-law Elizabeth had no children from her marriage, she looked after her niece and nephew.

Then at a reception Grand Duke Paul met Olga von Pistohlkors, the wife of Erich Gerhard von Pistohlkors, a captain in his regiment and aide-de-camp to his brother, Grand Duke Vladimir. Olga Karnovich, born in 1865 in St Petersburg, had married Erich in 1884 and was the mother of four children – one son and three daughters, the youngest born in 1890. Paul and Olga were so attracted to one another immediately that the imperial family, in order to avoid a scandal, had the Grand Duke transferred to the command of another regiment stationed far from St Petersburg. Despite this, they continued their relationship secretly and Paul, tormented by his sense of guilt, increasingly stayed away from his family and from his two children, who were living at their uncle Sergei's estate of Ilinskoye.

It is said that at a ball in the Winter Palace Olga von Pistohlkors wore a diamond necklace that Grand Duke Paul had inherited from his mother, Tsarina Maria Alexandrovna. It was recognized by his sister-in-law, the Dowager Empress Maria Feodorovna: offended by such a display, she asked her daughter-in-law, Tsarina Alexandra, to order Olga to leave the ball immediately. By the next day all of St Petersburg society had heard of the event. Captain von

Grand Duke Paul Alexandrovich in full dress uniform.

Pistohlkors found himself in the difficult situation of having to decide whether to resign his commission from the army or to divorce his wife. In the end he chose the second option. Olga then left the country for Italy.

In 1897, with the birth of their son Vladimir, the relationship between Grand Duke Paul and Olga von Pistohlkors became common knowledge.

Olga *c.* 1905, soon after she had been created Countess Hohenfelsen. She is wearing a five-strand pearl necklace.

It was tacitly accepted by the majority St Petersburg's high society, but not by the imperial family. Although Nicholas II remained fond of his uncle, he could not approve of the union, because it had done such damage to an existing marriage, and because Olga belonged to a lower social rank. Grand Duke Vladimir agreed with the Tsar, and was also deeply angry with his brother Paul for having destroyed the marriage of his aide-de-camp, Pistohlkors. Nicholas II placed a firm injunction against his uncle Paul marrying Olga on pain of losing all his imperial prerogatives – status, income, the right to live in Russia, and the custody of his own children.

The entire imperial family supported the hard line which the Tsar took in his role as head of the family. Grand Duke Sergei became the legal guardian of his niece Maria Pavlovna the Younger and his nephew Dmitri, and lavished love and attention on them. The deeply religious Grand Duchess Elizabeth could not accept her brother-in-law's behaviour.

In August 1902, the marriage of Grand Duchess Elena Vladimirovna to Prince Nicholas of Greece and Denmark was celebrated. This caused further tension and embarrassment for Grand Duke Paul, because the bridegroom was a brother of his late wife, Princess Alexandra. It was the first time that King George I of Greece had been in Russia since the death of his daughter Alexandra, and every effort was made to avoid an encounter between him and his son-in-law.

As the wedding celebrations ended, Paul took the decision to leave Russia. His brother Sergei and his sister-in-law Elizabeth implored him to reconsider, to think of his children and of his responsibilities in Russia, but Paul refused to yield to such pressure. An official of the court waited for him at the station to hand over enough money for the first stages of his journey. His destination was Italy, where Olga awaited him. In October 1902, in the Tuscan town of Livorno, he finally married Olga, in a Greek Orthodox ceremony. As he had contracted a morganatic marriage that was not authorized by the Tsar, Paul was banished from Russia, deprived of all his privileges, and had his property confiscated. (Nicholas's father, Alexander III, had taken a similarly severe position in 1891, when his cousin, Grand Duke Michael Mikhailovich, had committed the sin of contracting a morganatic marriage; the Grand Duke subsequently chose to live in England.) Paul subsequently wrote to his children Maria and Dmitri reassuring them that his feelings for them had not changed, but saying that, at the same time, he was not able to renounce his love for Olga. Not until a year after Paul's departure into exile were Maria and Dmitri allowed to see their father again.

Paul had purchased a mansion belonging to the Yusupovs in the elegant quarter of Boulogne-sur-Seine on the edge of Paris. In 1903 a second child was born – a girl, Irina [271]. Olga and her children had no titles, but in 1904 Luitpold, Prince Regent of Bavaria, created her Countess Hohenfelsen, with the right to pass on the Hohenfelsen title to her male descendants. In 1905 Paul and Olga's third child, Natalia, was born in Paris. The couple and their three children mixed freely in cosmopolitan Parisian society, even meeting members of the Russian aristocracy who frequently made pleasure trips to the French capital.

In 1905 Paul received news of the assassination of his brother Sergei (see p. 87). He was deeply affected, and obtained permission from the Tsar to return to Russia for six days to take part in the funeral. After the funeral, Paul asked the Tsar for permission to spend more time with his children. Grand Duchess Elizabeth, however, to whom the guardianship of the children had passed after the death of her husband [93], would not consent to this. Paul was now allowed to return occasionally to Russia accompanied by Olga, but he was not allowed to live there permanently.

Between the autumn of 1908 and the beginning of 1909, two further tragedies blighted the life of Grand Duke Paul, as his remaining brothers died within a few months of each other – Grand Duke Alexei in 1908 and

Grand Duke Vladimir in 1909. This meant that Paul was now the Tsar's only surviving uncle, and a senior member of the Romanov family. He was still in exile in Paris, but the time for reconciliation and for return to his native country was now approaching, not just for him, but also for Olga and their children.

When the couple lived in Paris, Grand Duke Paul and his wife frequently visited the shop of Cartier. In 1908, Paul ordered a tiara for Olga: it was composed of seven pear-shaped diamonds with a total weight of 121.42 carats, supported by an undulating line of diamonds; the central stone alone weighed 27 carats. He also ordered a *devant de corsage* of diamonds and pearls, which was decorated with three button pearls in a setting of brilliant-cut and French-cut diamonds, from which hung three drop pearls weighing 285 grains and an oval pearl weighing 185 grains [136].

In 1909 the Grand Duke placed another order, for a long necklace composed of a band of nine intertwined strands of pearls and a circular motif of diamonds with two crossed 'P's (for Paul) surmounted by the imperial Russian crown. The following year, this type of jewelry became highly fashionable and often had a drop pearl as the terminal decoration.

In 1911 the tiara made in 1908 was redesigned by Cartier: the seven pear-shaped diamonds were inserted within circles of brilliant-cut diamonds, in a design similar to that of the *kokoshnik* of Grand Duchess Vladimir [99]. Completely articulated, the tiara could be worn as a *devant de corsage*, and the detachable diamonds could be mounted as pendants on the edge of the circles. We can admire these splendid pieces of jewelry in a photograph taken at the Hungarian Ball organized by Madame de Yturbe in Paris in the summer of 1912 [136], where in addition she wears a *collier russe*, one of the pieces of jewelry that her husband had inherited from his mother, Tsarina Maria Alexandrovna.

Another order for Olga was placed with Cartier in 1912, this time for an elegant *parure* of diamonds and aquamarines in the fashionable style of the period, incorporating elements in Persian style [139–41]. It comprised an aigrette tiara, in which a pear-shaped aquamarine surmounted a design set with diamonds, and a feather could be inserted in the space behind the stone. There was also an elegant necklace composed of two strands of diamonds with a centrepiece decorated by a cushion-cut aquamarine from which was suspended a pear-shaped aquamarine; all the diamonds were mounted in a platinum millegrain setting. The *parure* was completed by a beautiful *devant de corsage*, which was also made from diamonds, with two

Opposite: Olga, Countess Hohenfelsen, with her son Vladimir in their home in Paris.

ABOVE: Olga, Countess Hohenfelsen (right), with the Infanta Eulalia of Spain at Madame de Yturbe's Hungarian Ball in Paris in 1912. She wears a dress by the couturier Worth; her 1911 Cartier tiara is worn as a *devant de corsage* with her five-strand pearl necklace, and her 1908 Cartier *devant de corsage* with its three drop pearls is mounted on a sable busby with another pearl supporting a large aigrette of white feathers. Around her neck she displays a fabulous *tiare russe*, inherited by Grand Duke Paul from his mother, Tsarina Maria Alexandrovna.

RIGHT: The mazurka was led by the Infante Don Luis (son of the Infanta Eulalia) and Princess Lucien Murat. The grandest personalities of Parisian high society took part in this highly original event, including the Duc and Duchesse de Morny and the Marquis de Talleyrand-Périgord.

Grand Duke Paul and Olga, Countess Hohenfelsen, *c.* 1912.

oval aquamarines and a pendant with a cushion-cut aquamarine encircled by diamond motifs.

This *parure* celebrated good fortune, as in January 1912 their banishment was lifted, and Paul and his family were able to return to live in Russia. Although the Grand Duke owned a palace in St Petersburg, he decided to live instead in Tsarskoe Selo. He commissioned a palace similar in style to their house in Paris, filled it with every modern comfort, and had the rooms designed to display his collection of art. The house was finished in May 1914. The Grand Duke and his family went to live there, unaware of the events which would unfold in the months to come.

The consort of Grand Duke Paul was still known as Countess Hohenfelsen. However, as Russia was drawn into war against Germany, it

ABOVE: The aigrette tiara from the *parure* designed by Cartier for Olga, Countess Hohenfelsen, in 1912, composed of diamonds and aquamarines mounted in platinum millegrain settings. The centre of the tiara is set with a cushion-cut aquamarine. Behind the pear-shaped aquamarine a feather could be inserted.

OVERLEAF, LEFT: The *devant de corsage* from the *parure*. The oval aquamarines could be detached to serve as brooches, and the pendant too could be worn separately.

OVERLEAF, RIGHT: The necklace from the *parure*. It is formed of two strands of diamonds; the centrepiece is a large cushion-cut aquamarine, from which a pear-shaped aquamarine surrounded by diamonds is suspended.

was no longer appropriate for the wife of a Russian Grand Duke to have a German title. Olga's marriage was morganatic, and she could not become a grand duchess, so in 1915 the Tsar conferred on her the status and name of Princess Paley; her children became Prince and Princess Paley. This was just in time for her son Vladimir's departure for the front.

Soon after the outbreak of the First World War, Princess Paley, with the support of the other three women living at Tsarskoe Selo, converted the ballroom of her palace into a hospital for soldiers wounded in the war. In her memoirs, Olga wrote of the terrible period of the Great War:

> At the start of the conflict, Grand Duke Paul was in command of the first corps of the Imperial Guard, and my son Vladimir, after twenty months spent in the trenches, had just been officially appointed to his father's service. In September 1916, after two years of uninterrupted work and struggle to obtain the necessary contributions and materials for the large reception centre made from the ballroom of our residence (that I had created in May 1914), and two months of war as I worked under the patronage of the Empress, my doctor advised me to take a period of rest. And so I went to the Crimea, where I experienced my last moments of true happiness with the arrival of my husband and my son.

After this brief family reunion, the situation continued to deteriorate irreversibly. Olga later recalled the terrible period in January 1918, when their home in Tsarskoe Selo was declared a 'museum of the people'. It was only because of the persistence of friends such as Alexander Polovstov and Monsieur Loukomsky that Olga was able to maintain ownership of the estate, the house, and all the objects it contained: 'Thus I acted as a guide to the civilian visitors, soldiers and sailors who would ask me for information about the art objects on display. Only a few would dare to make unpleasant remarks, saying that, before the revolution, all these treasures had been hidden from the people.'

In reality, the only riches that could have been hidden were the jewels and the precious objects which most members of the aristocracy and *haute bourgeoisie* had deposited in banks for fear of theft and looting of the palaces. But on 27 January 1918 the Bolshevik Government approved the confiscation of property held by the banks, and for many people this meant complete ruin. Even Grand Duke Paul had deposited all the jewelry he had inherited from his parents in a bank; fearing that his name might attract the attention and the greed of the revolutionaries, he had deposited the jewels – of which the total value seems to have been 50 million francs – in his wife's name. Olga wrote:

The family in 1916. From left to right: Olga, now Princess Paley, Irina, Vladimir (a soldier in the war), Natalia, and Grand Duke Paul.

> Some days later, Colonel Petrokov told me that he had been summoned to the bank in his capacity as the Grand Duke's administrator. He opened the boxes, which had been placed on a table, and before his eyes appeared necklaces, brooches, pendants, and tiaras made of pearls, diamonds, sapphires and emeralds. The radiance and sparkle of these fabulous jewels was such that the person inspecting the jewelry cried out 'This is what happened to our wealth! These belonged to Citizen Paley, but now we will take them all back.'

The jewels were then returned to their boxes, and the keys were given back to the administrator Petrokov, but it was known where the treasure was kept.

The end came for Grand Duke Paul at the beginning of 1919. On 28 January he and three other grand dukes were taken to the Fortress of SS. Peter and Paul and shut up in the dungeons. Two days later, at 3 o'clock in the morning, they were taken out into the Mint Square within the fortress, made to stand in line beside a deep common grave, and shot in the head.

Of all the magnificent pieces of jewelry that had belonged to Grand Duke Paul's family, the only one to reappear was the splendid *parure* of diamonds and aquamarines created by Cartier in 1912 [139–41]. It seems likely that this was not plundered with the rest of the treasure because Olga had kept it in her house in Paris.

The Yusupovs

Princess Zenaida Nikolaievna was the last of the historic dynasty of the Yusupovs. The daughter of Prince Nikolai Borisovich Yusupov and Countess Tatiana Alexandrovna de Ribaupierre, she was born on 2 October 1861, and was the only one of three children to survive – leaving her the richest heiress in Russia. She served as lady-in-waiting to the Empress Maria Feodorovna (and later to the Empress Alexandra), and was a close friend of Grand Duchess Elizabeth, whose country estate was near hers.

A reception had been organized at the behest of the Empress Maria Feodorovna to introduce Princess Zenaida to the Prince of Battenberg, but instead she met and fell in love with Count Felix Sumarokov-Elston, a lieutenant in the Horse Guards, grandson of Countess Tiesenhausen, at whose house the reception was held. He soon asked for her hand, and after an engagement lasting several years the couple married in the church of the Chevaliers Gardes in April 1882. Her father agreed that on his death her husband would take the Yusupov name and title. In 1883 their first child, Nikolai, was born, and he was followed by Felix in 1887. Nikolai died in 1908 in a duel provoked by a love affair, leaving his brother Felix as the heir.

The jewels belonging to the Yusupov family were among the most beautiful in Europe (Zenaida's father was a passionate collector of precious stones), and included several very famous diamonds and pearls. Of these, some survived the Revolution (for their rescue, see below). The Polar Star diamond [149, 157] is a splendid cushion-shaped stone weighing 41.285 carats, from the mines at Golconda in India. Its history is unknown before the period of its ownership by Napoleon's older brother, Joseph Bonaparte, and its subsequent purchase by Princess Tatiana Alexandrovna Yusupov, Zenaida's mother. The rose-coloured Ram's Head diamond, a 17.47-carat stone in the shape of a flattened octahedron, was a gift from Catherine the Great to her favourite, Prince Potemkin. The Sultan of Morocco is a steel-coloured cushion-cut diamond weighing 35.67 carats, in the possession of the Yusupovs since 1840. There were also earrings with pear-shaped diamonds said to have belonged to Queen Marie Antoinette of France [149].

Of pearls, the oval Régente [146–47, 149], weighing 302.78 grains, has a fascinating history. Napoleon I purchased it in 1811 from Nitot (forerunner of Chaumet) for the vast price of 40,000 francs, to celebrate the birth

Princess Zenaida Nikolaievna Yusupov, Countess Sumarokov-Elston, in her palace on the Moika Embankment in St Petersburg in 1914.

of his son, the King of Rome, and had it mounted as the central ornament of a tiara for the Empress Marie Louise; in 1853 it was removed and made into the central decoration of a large *devant de corsage* created by the court jeweller Lemonnier for Eugénie de Montijo on her marriage to Napoleon III [147]. In 1887 the French Government sold the crown jewels, and the *devant de corsage* was sold for 176,000 francs to a Monsieur J. Roussell, acting on behalf of Fabergé. Roussell brought it to St Petersburg, and Fabergé in turn sold it to Princess Zenaida Yusupov. A large tiara and a *parure* had been created to accompany the *devant de corsage*, including earrings set with two wonderful drop pearls [147]. These earrings seem to have been sold privately to Fabergé, perhaps directly from a representative of the Empress Eugénie, then in exile in England. (The Régente and the earrings survived the Revolution. When the Régente reappeared at auction at Christie's in Geneva on 12 May 1988 it was rumoured that the jewel had remained in the Yusupov Palace in Moscow, but it is more likely that it was taken out by the family. It is very probable that the earrings were acquired by Cartier after the Revolution and sold to a private collector; on 24–25 October 1990 they appeared at Sotheby's in New York in a sale of the collection of Isabel Van Wie Willys, without any indication of their outstanding provenance.)

Another historic pearl that was saved is the splendid La Pelegrina [150–51]. Weighing 133.16 grains and with a perfect pear shape, this jewel has a history that begins in the 17th century, when it is said to have been part

A photograph from an exhibition of Russian art held in London in 1935.
At the top is the pearl known as La Pelegrina. Another historic gem, the Azra
black pearl, hangs from a necklace composed of a string of pearls. Below is
an antique-cut diamond motif suspended below a black button pearl. Below left
and right are earrings of perfectly spherical pearls, each surmounted by a diamond.

Princess Zenaida Yusupov in the early 20th century, contemplating
La Pelegrina on a long string of pearls. She wears the pearl and diamond
earrings seen opposite.

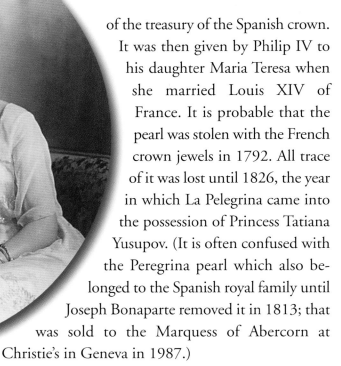

of the treasury of the Spanish crown. It was then given by Philip IV to his daughter Maria Teresa when she married Louis XIV of France. It is probable that the pearl was stolen with the French crown jewels in 1792. All trace of it was lost until 1826, the year in which La Pelegrina came into the possession of Princess Tatiana Yusupov. (It is often confused with the Peregrina pearl which also belonged to the Spanish royal family until Joseph Bonaparte removed it in 1813; that was sold to the Marquess of Abercorn at Christie's in Geneva in 1987.)

The vast collection of pearls outstanding for their beauty and historic importance also included the drop-shaped black pearl known as the Azra [150], which originally formed part of the Russian crown jewels. In 1783 it was given by Catherine the Great to her favourite, Prince Potemkin, and he bequeathed to his niece, Princess Tatiana. The same provenance was ascribed to a fantastic necklace formed of a string of thirty large perfectly matched black pearls. The necklace was accompanied by a pair of earrings, each formed of a round black pearl surmounted by a diamond.

Princess Zenaida's son, Prince Felix, was to add to the Yusupov jewels on his marriage. He was heir to the largest private fortune in Russia, with more than forty estates. His proposed marriage to the niece of Nicholas II, Irina Alexandrovna, only daughter of Grand Duchess Xenia and Grand Duke Alexander Mikhailovich, was opposed by her family because of his dissolute behaviour, but approval was finally given by the Dowager Empress Maria Feodorovna: Felix was the son of her dear friend Princess

ABOVE: Princess Irina Alexandrovna and Prince Felix Yusupov on the occasion of their engagement in 1913.

OPPOSITE: Chaumet's first design for a *devant de corsage* in diamonds and emeralds, part of a *parure* commissioned by Prince Felix Yusupov as one of his wedding presents for his wife. The upper element, with a large rectangular diamond, was changed in the executed version [*overleaf*].

OVERLEAF: Archive photographs from Chaumet of the diamond and emerald necklace, earrings and *devant de corsage* as realized.

1 <u>extra</u> 3
2 - 1
3 - 2

1

2

3

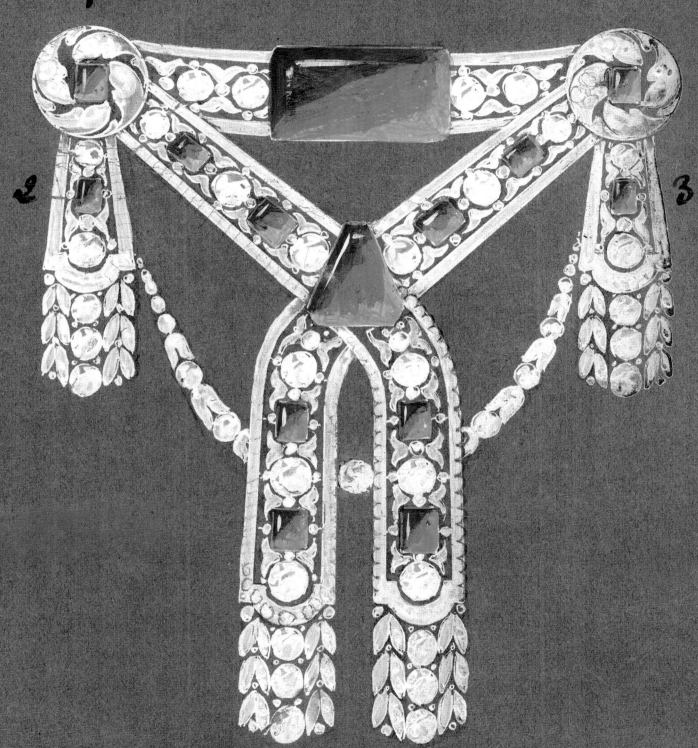

OPPOSITE: A preparatory design proposed to Prince Felix by Chaumet for a garland style *devant de corsage* in rubies and diamonds, including the Polar Star diamond in the centre.

Zenaida, and it was arranged that she should meet him in Denmark to decide the future of her favourite granddaughter. Felix, using all his charm, convinced her. Irina and Felix were engaged in 1913, and on 22 February 1914 they were married in the chapel of the Anichkov Palace, the residence of the Dowager Empress.

As Felix was not of royal blood, Irina had to renounce her right to the throne. Thus to her great relief on the day of the wedding she was excused from wearing the jewels and heavy mantle required for grand duchesses. Instead, she wore a white dress with a train embroidered with silver; her lace veil, worn previously by her mother, was held in place by a tiara created by Cartier in 1911, decorated with engraved rock crystal and diamonds, the centrepiece of which was a circular-cut diamond weighing 3.66 carats, a gift to her from Princess Zenaida. The bride was accompanied by the Tsar, followed by the Dowager Empress with Grand Duke Alexander Mikhailovich. After the ceremony, a reception was organized for a few close friends in the winter garden of the Palace, and there Grand Duchess Xenia gave her daughter a diamond and emerald brooch which she herself had received as a wedding present from her husband, while Maria Feodorovna gave her a diamond and pearl brooch.

Before their marriage, Prince Felix had taken certain important pieces of jewelry and stones to Chaumet in Paris so that they could be redesigned for her. Amongst many *parures* [154–55], he commissioned one in emeralds, which consisted of a necklace in which the emeralds were mounted in Russian style with a ring of very small diamonds within a border of much larger diamonds, alternating with a circular design in diamonds; pendant earrings; and a large *devant de corsage*. In the original design for the *devant de corsage* [153], preserved in the Chaumet archives, the upper part was decorated by a large rectangular step-cut emerald: this was replaced in the final version by a garland of diamonds, and itself became the centrepiece of a bandeau which also incorporated diamonds. The other *parures* included an important tiara and a *devant de corsage* in rubies and diamonds, a necklace terminating in two tassels of rubies and diamonds, and a long necklace of cabochon sapphires and diamonds which anticipated the *sautoirs* that became fashionable in the 1920s.

In December 1916 Prince Felix became involved with something far removed from commissioning fine jewelry, when he and Grand Duke Dmitri Pavlovich, the son of Grand Duke Paul, resorted to murder to rid

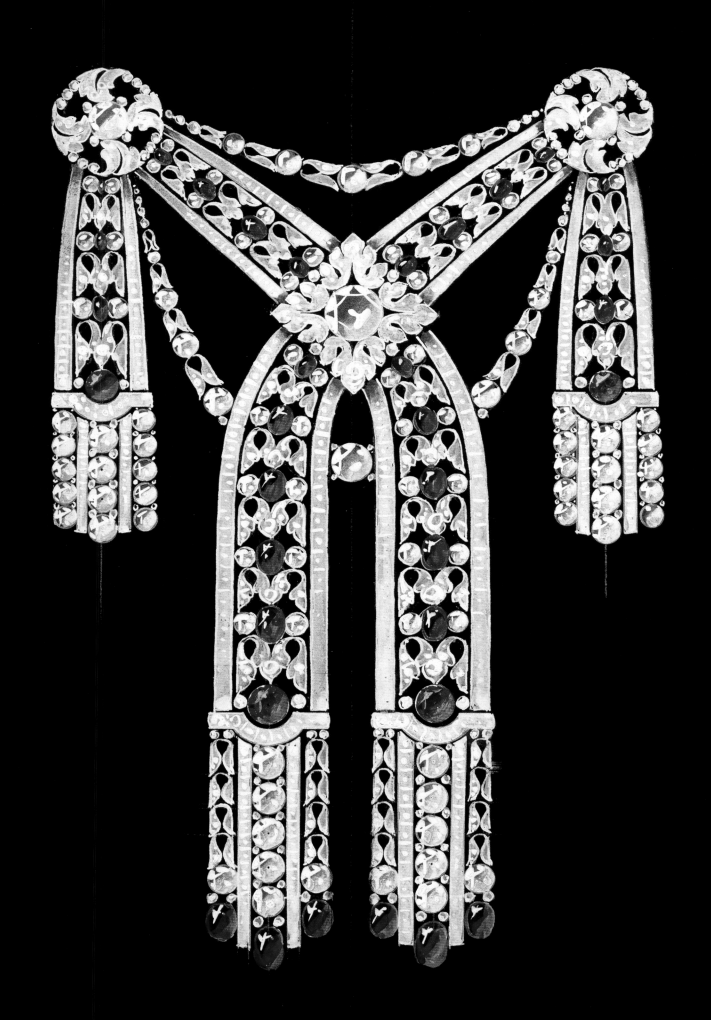

the imperial family of the much hated influence that the monk Rasputin wielded over the Tsarina (see pp. 225–26).

At the beginning of the Revolution in 1917 there was systematic looting of many palaces of the nobility, and Prince Felix decided to hide the collection. We can only imagine how he managed to take the jewelry of his mother Zenaida and his wife Irina, together with the splendid jewelry given to his mother-in-law, Grand Duchess Xenia, by her parents at her marriage, which he had to collect from her residence – presumably with the help of one of his brothers-in-law – to Moscow. The ancient Yusupov Palace there [260, 261] had many underground passages, and Felix, with the assistance of a faithful servant, walled up what had been saved of the family's treasures in the hope of retrieving them in better times to come. (For the tragic end of the story, see below, pp. 260–66.) The only jewels retained by his mother and his wife were their strings of pearls and the few historic gems that we met above – the Polar Star [149, 157], Ram's Head and Sultan of Morocco diamonds as well as the Marie Antoinette diamond earrings [149], and of pearls the Régente [146–47, 149] and La Pelegrina [150–51] and the collection of wonderful black pearls including the Azra [150].

Later, during his exile, Prince Felix sold the diamonds to Cartier. He parted with the Sultan of Morocco in 1924, and it went to a buyer in America in the late 1920s. Negotiations for the Polar Star began in 1924, but Cartier did not gain possession until 1928; they sold it to Lydia, Lady Deterding. The diamond earrings of Marie Antoinette went to Marjorie Merriweather Post. Cartier bought the Ram's Head in 1927 and sold it to Daisy Fellowes; it was stolen in 1939 and has never reappeared. Of the Yusupov pearls, after its display in a great exhibition of Russian art in London in 1935 the necklace with the Azra pearl was bought by Lady Deterding; sadly she lost the pearl somewhere in Paris, and it too has never reappeared. Prince Yusupov also sold the splendid black pearl necklace to Cartier, but he kept La Pelegrina until 1953, when he finally parted with it to the jeweller Jean Lombard.

Opposite: A preparatory design proposed by Chaumet to Prince Felix for a *devant de corsage* in rubies and diamonds.

The Duchess of Leuchtenberg

The House of Leuchtenberg originated with Eugène de Beauharnais, the son of Josephine and Alexandre, Vicomte de Beauharnais. When Josephine married Napoleon, Eugène was adopted by the future Emperor. In 1806 he married Princess Amalia of Bavaria, daughter of Maximilian I, and the King conferred on him the title of Duke of Leuchtenberg. The couple had seven children, the last of whom, Prince Maximilian de Beauharnais, married Grand Duchess Maria Nikolaievna, the eldest daughter of Tsar Nicholas I; as a result, he became Prince Romanovsky and Imperial Highness. From that time onward, dukes of Leuchtenberg were also called Romanovsky princes – eventually becoming a cadet branch of the imperial family – and they lived permanently in Russia in a splendid residence that was to become known after Grand Duchess Maria as the Mariinsky Palace. The palace had been built by the Tsar for his beloved daughter to the design of the architect Andrei Stakenschneider, and the couple took up residence in 1845.

The Grand Duchess died in 1873. In 1878 her son Prince Eugene Maximilianovich Romanovsky, 5th Duke of Leuchtenberg, married as his second wife Zenaida Dmitrievna, youngest of the three sisters of General Mikhail Dmitrievich Skobelev. After her marriage she became Comtesse de Beauharnais, and in 1899 she received the *ad personam* title of Duchess of Leuchtenberg.

In 1884 three of the Grand Duchess's children came to live in the palace with their families as an economy measure; but the building was subsequently sold to the Treasury, and, retaining its name of Mariinsky, became the seat of the Imperial Council and the Council of Ministers.

Like all the members of the Romanov family, the dukes of Leuchtenberg owned an important collection of jewelry. They saved it by fleeing to Bavaria, thus avoiding the violent events of the Revolution. In the 1920s their jewels were sold in Switzerland to the jeweller Seiler of Vevey, and still today important pieces appear in international auctions.

OPPOSITE: A magnificent diamond tiara designed by Fabergé *c.* 1890, with the mark of the master August Holmström. A series of arches increase in size towards the centre; the diamonds are mounted on a knife-edge setting, each central pear-shaped diamond flanked by briolette-cut diamonds. According to Leuchtenberg family tradition, it was known as the Empress Josephine's Tiara, because the briolette-cut diamonds had been a gift from Tsar Alexander I to the Empress Josephine. It is said that the Tsar was in the habit of taking her presents when he visited her in the Château of Malmaison after her divorce from Napoleon.

OPPOSITE: A large *devant de corsage* with a hexagonally cut emerald encircled by diamonds as the centrepiece, surrounded by a leaf design and cabochon emeralds, with a pendant pear-shaped cabochon emerald.

LEFT: An antique brooch with three flowers mounted *en tremblant*, which can be transformed into a tiara. The smaller flowers have a central cushion-cut diamond encircled with emeralds, and petals set with diamonds; the largest one has a hexagonally cut emerald at its centre and petals made from diamonds and emeralds. The flowers are surrounded by flexible tassels in diamonds and emeralds.

BELOW: A tiara in emeralds and diamonds dating from *c*. 1830 (kept in a box from the famous Parisian jeweller Mellerio). Wild roses in diamonds are accompanied by cushion-cut emeralds, mounted in gold. The tiara can be disassembled into at least three brooches.

ABOVE: A necklace of alternating oval and lozenge motifs from which hang eleven pear-shaped cabochon emeralds encircled by diamonds, mounted in gold and silver, from the second half of the 19th century (photographed in three sections, the central part at the top). It was worn in a number of ways by the Duchess of Leuchtenberg. The emeralds were subsequently returned to the Imperial Treasury; it is likely that they had been given to the Leuchtenberg family, who sent them back to the Imperial Cabinet at the outbreak of war in 1914.

OPPOSITE, LEFT: The Duchess in boyar costume, wearing the necklace as a stomacher. Just visible bottom left is her diamond and emerald *kokoshnik*.

OPPOSITE, ABOVE: The Duchess wearing a coronet created from the diamond sections of her necklace [*cf.* 105].

OPPOSITE, BELOW: The Duchess, with the emerald necklace decorating her dress, wearing the *kokoshnik* and a necklace of emerald and diamond clusters.

Mathilde Kschessinska & The Romanovs

Mathilde Felixovna Kschessinska enjoyed a twenty-five-year-long career as a prima ballerina with the Russian Imperial Ballet in St Petersburg, in the legendary Mariinsky Theatre, but little is known about her true artistic talents, because after the Revolution everything to do with the life of the former mistress of Tsar Nicholas II – documents, articles, memoirs – was deliberately destroyed. The Bolshevik government regarded her as an outstanding symbol of tsarist corruption, and it was no accident, but a deliberate insult, that Lenin made his first speech from the balcony of a bedroom in Mathilde's splendid villa [174–75], which had already been looted.

Her relationship with the Tsarevich had been encouraged by his father, Alexander III (see p. 20). In her memoirs, Mathilde recalls meeting the Tsarevich at a dance recital in the theatre school. It was traditional for the imperial family to attend this annual event at the academy, in which the best students took part. Even before watching the dancers take to the stage, the Tsar, in a breach of etiquette, asked to be introduced to Kschessinska, and during the lunch that followed the performance he invited the young dancer to sit beside him and reserved the other chair next to her for the Tsarevich, saying: 'Please, not too much flirting!' Thus began a love affair which involved them deeply for many years. Nicholas presented Kschessinska with a palace at 18 Angliisky Prospekt which had been Rimsky-Korsakov's residence, and the prima ballerina lived there with her sister. (Later she acquired the splendid villa at 2/4 Bolshaya Dvoryanskaya.)

Even when their relationship had come to an end, Nicholas remained very fond of the famous ballerina, so much so that it is rumoured that although he was married, he continued to meet her in secret. Mathilde was able to maintain good relations with the imperial family and could count on the protection of various grand dukes, including Sergei Mikhailovich. Sergei gave Mathilde a dacha in the little town of Strelna near St Petersburg, where in the summer she received her friends and numerous acquaintances. She also began a relationship with Grand Duke Andrei Vladimirovich, seven years her junior (his father, Grand Duke Vladimir, was President of the

Opposite: Mathilde Kschessinska, wearing a wonderful circular-cut diamond *rivière* necklace with earrings *en suite*, an early gift from the Tsarevich. On her headband she has another necklace [*see* 173], with a ribbon and bow design, probably by Fabergé, which seems to have been one of her favourite pieces of jewelry: its centrepiece, a large bow above a pear-shaped diamond, could be detached and worn as a brooch.

Academy of Russian Art, upon which the Mariinsky Theatre was dependent). In 1903 at Strelna Mathilde gave birth to her only son: called Vladimir in honour of his grandfather, he was always known in the family as Vova.

Mathilde was considered to be one of the most elegant women in St Petersburg. Her love of furs was legendary, from eyecatching ermine overcoats to long cloaks of dark brown sable, and she often bought dozens of outfits from the finest Parisian couturiers. Her particular preference, however, was for jewelry. Her close friendship with Agathon Fabergé, son of the famous Carl, meant that Mathilde was able to choose jewels for herself. At Vova's baptism, Grand Duke Vladimir presented her with a beautiful cross of emeralds from the Urals. She also had a splendid diamond *rivière* necklace given to her by the Tsarevich. Her favourite piece was a necklace that she was often photographed wearing: probably created by Fabergé, it was designed with ribbons and bows set with diamonds and had a centrepiece in the form of a bow with a large pear-shaped diamond which could be detached and worn as a brooch [167, 173].

When the career of a star dancer had lasted for a decade, it was customary for gifts to be presented by admirers and by the Tsar. The latter generally gave a ballerina an imperial eagle in gold or silver (depending on her importance as an artist) set with coloured stones, while a male dancer received a gold watch. As Mathilde's tenth anniversary, in 1901, approached, she sent a message to the Tsar via Grand Duke Sergei Mikhailovich that she would prefer a different type of gift, and she received a brooch with a cabochon sapphire encircled by a serpent set with diamonds.

In 1911, for her twentieth anniversary, Mathilde received from the Tsar an eagle in diamonds mounted in platinum with a pink sapphire as a pendant. At the request of Grand Duke Andrei, Prince Alexander Constantinovich Shervashidze, who was also a famous scenographer, designed a bandeau in diamonds with six large cabochon sapphires. This was officially made by Fabergé, but the work was probably executed by the atelier of August Holmström and August Hollming, who specialized in working with platinum and diamonds. The bandeau was made to match a piece of jewelry Mathilde had already received from Grand Duke Andrei. Created by Fabergé, this consisted of a pendant with a large cabochon sapphire

OPPOSITE: Tsarevich Nicholas Alexandrovich in civilian dress.

OVERLEAF, LEFT: Mathilde Kschessinska in the title role of *La Fille du Pharaon*, wearing a fabulous display of diamonds.

OVERLEAF, BACKGROUND IMAGE: The Mariinsky Theatre in St Petersburg.

Helene de Mrozovsky

St. Pétersbourg
Nevsky 20

weighing more than 100 carats, from which a pear-shaped cabochon sapphire weighing 83 carats was suspended; both stones were mounted in platinum and encircled by diamonds. For the same anniversary, Grand Duke Sergei Mikhailovich gave her a jewel box made by Fabergé of rare wood mounted in gold; the box contained a collection of yellow diamonds of different sizes, which the ballerina was to take to the court jeweller for them to be made into a brooch. This she did, and the resulting brooch was especially beautiful.

In 1917, General Vladislav Halle, Commander of the Fourth District of Petrograd, warned Mathilde that she should leave the city, because hostile popular feeling might at any moment become dangerous for her and for her family. She last appeared on the stage of the Mariinsky Theatre on 2 February, when she danced the role of Columbine in *Carnival*, in a performance to raise funds for wounded soldiers. On 22 February Mathilde gave a farewell party in her palace. The Revolution began on the 23rd, and five days later, after eight o'clock in the evening, the woman who had been so adored by the Tsar, dressed in a plain coat and with a scarf on her head in order not to be recognized, left her palace in secret with her son Vova, Peter Vladimirov, and two other friends. She took with her only a few pieces of jewelry from her immense collection. The next day, her housekeeper opened the doors of her palace to the revolutionaries, allowing its devastation.

Mathilde found refuge in the home of a friend, where she remained hidden for several days. On 2 March, Nicholas II abdicated, bringing the Romanov dynasty to an end, and initiating the persecution of people who had been prominent figures in the *ancien régime*.

Mathilde and Vova were finally reunited with Andrei in the Crimea. In 1919 the three of them managed to escape and reached the south of France. The death of Grand Duchess Vladimir a year later left Mathilde and Andrei free, and they married in the Russian Orthodox Church in Cannes on 30 January 1921. Andrei's brother Cyril proclaimed himself head of the imperial family (although this was disputed by the rest of the Romanovs), and made the marriage even more respectable by conferring the title of Princess Krasinsky on Mathilde, a title that could be inherited by her son. Andrei wrote to the Dowager Empress Maria Feodorovna, living in Denmark with her daughter Olga. The latter sent the following message: 'The Dowager Empress is in favour of this union and sends her good wishes.'

OPPOSITE: Mathilde Kschessinska in stage costume, wearing her necklace with diamond bows [*cf.* 167] and a *collier de chien* of diamond-set interlaced circles. Both are likely to be have been designed by Fabergé. Numerous brooches, all of which were gifts from her admirers, are pinned to her clothes.

BELOW: Mathilde Kschessinska in her drawing room, wearing her favourite ribbon and bow necklace. The decoration of the room reflects the revival of interest in Neoclassicism that characterized many elegant buildings of this period in the city.

Mathilde Kschessinska's villa at 2/4 Bolshaya Dvoryanskaya in St Petersburg,
built at the beginning of the 20th century by Alexander von Gogen, seen from
Kronverksky Avenue. The large Art Nouveau-style windows on the right lit the
winter garden. (The house is now the State Museum of Political History of
Russia, and its address is Ulitsa Kuybysheva.)

❧ 3 ❧

JEWELLED STARS

Among the important ladies of the turn of the century, four stand out for their personalities, their important jewelry collections, and their connection with Russia and members of the imperial family: Crown Princess Marie of Romania, Princess Marthe Lucile Bibesco, the Marchioness of Ripon, and Nancy Leeds, Princess Anastasia of Greece.

Marie of Romania

Marie of Romania is one of the most romantic figures of the 20th century. The granddaughter of Alexander II and of Queen Victoria, she married Prince Ferdinand of Romania in 1893 (see p. 77) and became Queen of Romania in 1914. Her residence, the Cotroceni Palace, given to her in 1896 by her husband, was situated on the outskirts of Bucharest in a magnificent park. She much preferred it to her palace in the capital, the Palatul Victoriei, with its sombre formal rooms which she described as having not a single 'cosy corner'.

Marie spent many hours in her large Byzantine-style room there [179] with its green and gold wall decoration, surrounded by sculptures, which reflects something of her singular personality. Her favourite emblem, the cross, sparkled from the ceiling, was suspended from the chandeliers, painted on the ornate panelling, sculpted in stone, embroidered on the fabrics covering the furniture, and even on the wall hangings. The eye was

OPPOSITE: Princess Marie of Romania wearing jewelry including a tiara decorated with diamonds and pearls and a pendant Greek cross.

ABOVE: An antique pendant with an irregularly shaped cabochon sapphire, encircled by a gold serpent set with diamonds. Princess Marie inherited it from her grandfather, Tsar Alexander II.

Princess Marie in the uniform of a colonel of the 4th 'Rosiori' Hussars, reviewing a picket of Hussars.

constantly surprised as it discovered the many permutations of this very Byzantine motif. Superb bearskins from the Carpathian Mountains on the tiled floor completed the decoration of this evocative space.

An experienced horsewoman, she loved to go for long rides. She also liked to wear the costume of the Danubian peasant women, studded with silver and adorned with red stars.

Aside from her preference for all things Byzantine, Marie was particularly fond of the Pre-Raphaelites and of all art which expressed the liveliness of the soul through an elegant simplicity of form. She held performances by an orphanage at the Cotroceni Palace, on one occasion playing the role of a fairytale princess in a piece she herself had written. In the winter of 1896, she organized a memorable costume ball for the visit of her sister Victoria Melita, at which both appeared as the 'Distant Princess', a character created by the French dramatist Edmond Rostand in his play *La Princesse Lointaine* and made famous by the actress Sarah Bernhardt. Princess Marie described the clothes as follows: 'Ducky and I had chosen the same costume, the only difference being that hers was white with large white lilies pinned above her ears, while mine was black, and instead of the lilies I had red roses in my hair.'

Marie adored jewelry, which she wore in great quantities. One of the most beautiful pieces in her collection was a tiara in diamonds and pearls surmounted by a row of pear-shaped pearls [176]. She was often photographed wearing outstanding jewelry, including a large *devant de corsage* formed of a diamond and gemstone cluster from which was suspended an Orthodox cross set with precious stones, diamonds and pear-shaped pearls; a tiara of interlaced circles set in diamonds; and long strings of pearls. At the outbreak of the First World War, Marie – now Queen – decided to send the Romanian jewels and the most important pieces from her collection to Russia, thinking they would be safer there. Alas, they suffered the same fate as many other important collections, and vanished.

Marie loved to arrange flowers to decorate the Cotroceni Palace. The central photograph shows her in her beloved Byzantine-style room there.

Princess Marthe Lucile Bibesco

Marthe Lucile Lahovary, the third child of Ioan Lahovary and Emma Lahovary (née Princess Emma Mavrocordato), was born in 1886 in Bucharest. On 29 June 1902, she married Prince George III Valentin Bibesco, a scion of one of the most prestigious aristocratic families of Romania. (The Bibescu or Bibesco family enjoyed almost royal status, so much so that when the Romanian Liberal Party had proposed a national candidate for the throne in preference to the Hohenzollern prince who became Carol I – the father of Princess Marie's husband Ferdinand – they suggested Prince Nicholas, Prince George's uncle; he declined the offer.) Princess Marie sent Marthe her best wishes for the wedding and presented her with a star-shaped diamond brooch. The young bride looked particularly beautiful, as she wore a high *kokoshnik* encrusted with precious stones which had been a gift and a sparkling emerald necklace that set off the colour of her large green eyes.

S. A. S.

La Princesse Marthe Lucile Bibesco

PRECEDING PAGES, LEFT: Marthe Lucile Lahovary photographed on the day of her wedding to Prince George Bibesco in 1902. She is wearing a high *kokoshnik* decorated with a garland-style diamond necklace, hung with pear-shaped emeralds; a large cabochon emerald encircled with diamonds is set in the centre. Around her neck are a high *collier de chien* formed of strands of pearls with a centrepiece of diamonds and coloured stones, and a necklace made from garlands of diamonds from which five large circular cabochon emeralds are suspended.

PRECEDING PAGES, RIGHT: Princess Bibesco wearing a garland-style necklace in diamonds and emeralds and a tiara made of five large cabochon emeralds linked by festoons of diamonds. Both pieces could be worn as a necklace or as a tiara.

Marthe spent long periods in Paris, where she soon distinguished herself in the salons of high society among literary and political elites. Her favourite associates were Bertrand de Fénelon, a friend of Marcel Proust, and Elisabeth de Clermont-Tonnerre, who was known as 'the Intellectual Duchess'.

In 1903 her only daughter, Valentine, was born. Despite becoming a mother and having a wide circle of friends, Marthe felt bored, and neglected by her husband. It was thus with great enthusiasm that she welcomed the idea of accompanying him on a diplomatic mission to the Shah of Persia in 1905. (It may be presumed that this commission did not come by chance, as Marthe's father was Foreign Minister at the time.) They and five more people – accompanied by two skilled mechanics – made the journey in a grand 40cc Mercedes (driven by Prince George), a much smaller Mercedes, and an even smaller Fiat. Marthe kept a diary, which she wrote up as a manuscript entitled *Les Huit Paradis* ('The Eight Paradises'); two distinguished French friends supported its publication as a book, and with its successful appearance in 1908 she was launched on a career as a highly esteemed author of both novels and non-fiction.

On 24 March 1913 a concert was organized in the Cotroceni Palace. Princess Bibesco had recently returned from abroad and brought news of the French political situation. In the absence of Princess Marie, she accompanied Prince Ferdinand to the concert, wearing a magnificent black

OPPOSITE: A unique *devant de corsage*-cum-necklace in pearls, enamels and diamonds, with the monogram of Marthe Lucile Bibesco surmounted by a crown. Three strands of pearls form the necklace, together with two enamel and diamond sections at the sides, and a single strand of pearls crosses over the back of the neck and falls over the front to terminate at the brooch. The centrepiece hangs from the brooch and is decorated with translucent light pink enamel and a triple garland of pendant pearls.

DIAMANT OFFERT PAR
L'EMPEREUR NAPOLEON Ier
A
EMILIE PRINCESSE DE CHIMAY
APPORTE DE SAINTE HELENE
PAR LE COMTE DE LAS CASES
EN 1817

ABOVE: Princess Marthe Bibesco had what was known in her family as the 'St Helena Diamond' set by Cartier *c.* 1913 in a diamond pendant. The historic stone was believed to have been sent in 1817 by Napoleon I, in exile on the island of St Helena, to Emilie de Pellapra, later Princesse de Chimay (his supposed illegitimate daughter) – Princess Valentine Bibesco's mother.

OPPOSITE: A portrait of Princess Marthe Bibesco, painted by Giovanni Boldini in 1911. The Princess is wearing her garland-style diamond and pear-shaped cabochon emerald necklace as a tiara.

OFFERT PAR L'EMPEREUR NAPOLÉON 1ER
À SON RETOUR DE L'ÎLE D'ELBE 1815
À MADAME EMILIE DE PELLAPRA

velvet dress that set off the splendour of her diamond and emerald jewelry. The British legation, led by the Government Minister Sir George Barclay, included Colonel Christopher Thomson, who had just been transferred from Serbia. Marthe's arrival in the concert hall on the arm of the Crown Prince captured everyone's attention. That Christopher Thomson was entranced by her beauty soon became obvious to the other guests: Elise Batrianu, a friend of Marthe's, observed that 'That elegant English colonel may go cross-eyed just from looking at you', provoking the Princess's mirth. After the concert Colonel Thomson was presented to Marthe and fell in love with her at once, a feeling that he never lost, writing of it later in a book entitled *Smaranda*, dedicated to her, explaining that the heroine's name, 'Smaranda', which means 'emerald', was the name of a Byzantine princess, whose effigy was depicted in a stained-glass window in Constantinople.

Several pieces of jewelry in the family were traditionally believed to have been gifts of the Emperor Napoleon I [184, 186, 189]. In 1921 Princess Bibesco published the novel *Une Fille Inconnue de Napoléon* ('An Unknown Daughter of Napoleon') about the life of Emilie de Pellapra, who became the Princesse de Chimay. Born in Lyons in 1806, she was thought to be one of Napoleon I's illegitimate children. Widowed by Count Louis-Marie de Brigode, in 1830 she married the Prince de Chimay, with whom she had four children. Her fourth child, Valentine, married as her second husband Prince George Bibesco, and became the mother-in-law of Marthe Bibesco, inspiring the writer to tell Emilie de Pellapra's story. The book included a photograph of a bracelet which was said by her family to have been a gift sent by Napoleon to Emilie after his return from the island of Elba [186]. The bracelet was then passed on to her daughter and via Valentine to Marthe Bibesco. In fact, both the story of Emilie de Pellapra and her bracelet date from the post-Napoleonic era.

Unlike Queen Marie, who mistakenly chose to move her jewelry for safety to Petrograd (as St Petersburg had been renamed), Princess Bibesco deposited the famous Bibesco emeralds with the French legation in Bucharest, whence they were sent via diplomatic routes to the French

OPPOSITE, ABOVE: Princess Marthe Bibesco seen leaning on one of the automobiles of her husband, Prince George, who is seated at the steering wheel. Beside her is her mother-in-law, Princess Valentine Bibesco; behind Prince George is his sister Elise.

OPPOSITE, BELOW: A bracelet given to Marthe by her mother-in-law, Princess Valentine Bibesco. Traditionally it was held to have been a present from Napoleon I to Princess Valentine's mother, Emilie de Pellapra, later Princesse de Chimay, but in style it is later than 1815.

A gold, sapphire and diamond bracelet given
to Princess Elise Bibesco – Marthe Bibesco's
sister-in-law – by her mother, Princess Valentine.
It too was passed on with the legend that it had
been a gift from the Emperor Napoleon to his
daughter Emilie de Pellapra, later Princesse
de Chimay – Princess Valentine's mother.

Ambassador to the Russian court, Maurice Paléologue, locked in the
Embassy's safe, later transported to Paris, and returned safely to Marthe
at the end of the War.

In September 1916 Princess Bibesco undertook a journey to Russia,
where she was the guest of Maurice Paléologue. In Petrograd she met
Victoria Melita, Queen Marie's favourite sister, who had in the meantime
become the wife of Grand Duke Cyril Vladimirovich. Marthe and Victoria
Melita visited Tsarskoe Selo, where Grand Duchess Vladimir, Victoria
Melita's mother-in-law, revealed her concern at the worrying influence
exerted by the monk Rasputin on the Empress. In her diary Marthe wrote
about her visit to Petrograd:

> The city is in chaos. It is a charged atmosphere; in contrast to the
> opulence of shops, the streets overflow with uncollected rubbish.
> I was also told that there is no longer enough firewood and that
> food is becoming scarce. Every day there is a demonstration about
> something and all sorts of rumours abound. Where will it all end?

Not long afterwards, the revolutionaries were powerful enough to
force Tsar Nicholas II to abdicate. Returning to Bucharest, Princess Bibesco
became a nurse in Hospital 118, and won general admiration for her
tireless work.

OPPOSITE: Diamond jewelry from the collection of Princess Marthe Bibesco's
sister-in-law, Princess Elise Bibesco, who married Prince Barbu Stirbey. The
inset photograph shows Princess Elise wearing the necklace as a *kokoshnik*,
together with the earrings seen bottom left, and several strings of pearls.

Lady De Gray, Marchioness of Ripon

Constance Gladys De Gray was the daughter of Sidney Herbert, Secretary of War during the Crimean War. She was first married to the Earl of Lonsdale, and then from 1885 to Lord De Gray; her second marriage brought her the title of the Marchioness of Ripon when her father-in-law died in 1909. At the end of the 19th century, Gladys De Gray was a prominent figure in the cosmopolitan drawing rooms of the European aristocracy. She had a great talent for socializing and entertaining, and in 1911, as Marchioness of Ripon, she organized a memorable evening in her country house of Coombe Court in honour of the Dowager Empress Maria Feodorovna of Russia and her sister Alexandra, mother of King George V. Through her, the Hon. Albert Stopford met the most prominent figures in St Petersburg society, notably Grand Duchess Vladimir and Prince Felix Yusupov (see pp. 128–29), and became established in Russia.

She was a lover of all the arts, but her particular passion was for opera. At Covent Garden she introduced the great soprano Nellie Melba, and – significantly in the present context – she organized visits by Diaghilev's Ballets Russes. The first gala evening was held on 26 June 1911 in the presence of George V and Queen Mary, as part of the celebrations for their coronation. The performance was so spectacular that it definitively established both the Marchioness and the Ballets Russes.

Both as Lady De Gray and as the Marchioness of Ripon this enlightened patron was particularly fond of jewelry. She entrusted most of her commissions to Cartier in Paris, but both she and her second husband were also enthusiastic collectors of *objets de vertu* created by Fabergé, who had opened a branch of his company in New Bond Street in London.

OPPOSITE: A superb *collier de chien* created by Cartier in 1901 for Lady De Gray in typical garland style, with intertwined ribbons and flowers. The centrepiece is a bow with similar decoration which can be detached and worn as a brooch.

BELOW: The Marchioness of Ripon – as she had become – photographed in 1909 by Baron Adolf de Meyer. She is wearing the *collier de chien* seen opposite, and a diamond tiara in the shape of a *kokoshnik*.

Nancy Leeds, Princess Anastasia of Greece

Daughter of William Charles Stewart and Mary Holden Stewart of Cleveland, Ohio, the future Princess Anastasia of Greece was born Nancy May Stewart in 1883. She had been married twice before: she divorced her first husband, but her second husband, William B. Leeds, a steel magnate, on his death in 1908 left her an immense fortune.

In 1913 she moved to London, where she soon became part of high society and was celebrated for her extraordinary collection of jewels, which included exceptional emeralds that rivalled in splendour those of Grand Duchess Vladimir. In that social world, Nancy Leeds met Prince Christopher of Greece and Denmark, the brother of King Constantine I of Greece. Although she was eight years his senior, a relationship developed between the two of them which eventually led to marriage in 1920, in the Russian church in Vevey, Switzerland (Nancy had by then

converted to Greek Orthodoxy). Nancy at once received the name and title of Her Royal Highness, the Princess Anastasia of Greece. The couple then moved to London where they lived in Spencer House, and the British capital became the background to their intense social life. After only three years of marriage, however, Nancy became ill, and she died in 1923 at the age of forty.

OPPOSITE: Mrs W. B. Leeds, photographed *c.* 1913 wearing her diamond and pearl tiara from Cartier and two exceptional strings of Oriental pearls.

ABOVE: Two views of the tiara ordered by Nancy Leeds from Cartier in 1913. Interlacing circles in diamonds are bordered with seed pearls; within them, pear-shaped diamonds are suspended alternately with drop pearls; the central diamond weighed 21.60 carats. The design was clearly inspired by Grand Duchess Maria Pavlovna's *kokoshnik* [99].

ABOVE: Nancy Leeds and Prince Christopher of Greece photographed at their wedding in 1920, with his mother, Queen Olga (born Grand Duchess Olga Constantinovna of Russia). Nancy Leeds – now Princess Anastasia of Greece – is wearing jewelry designed by Cartier, seen above and opposite.

TOP: The bandeau tiara that held Princess Anastasia's veil in place has a row of circular diamonds framed by a lily of the valley design also set in diamonds.

OPPOSITE: The Princess's necklace, ordered in 1919, and brooch, *c.* 1910. The necklace, which could be worn in various lengths, comprises circular-cut diamonds alternating with hexagonally cut diamonds and has as its centrepiece a cushion-cut diamond with a suspended pear-shaped diamond. The wonderful bow-shaped brooch has two pear-shaped diamonds suspended from it.

~4~

St Petersburg and Paris

Paris was always a place of delight for Russian grand dukes and duchesses and aristocrats, and in the years from around 1890 to the eve of the First World War the 'City of Light' offered beautiful entertainers who travelled back and forth to Russia, welcomed the Ballets Russes, and devised parties that inspired similar grand exotic gatherings in St Petersburg.

Two women embodied the period: the Spanish dancer Caroline Otero and the Italian Lina Cavalieri, who was considered to be the most beautiful woman in the world at the start of the 20th century. 'La Belle Otero' [198–201] was literally covered with jewelry by her many lovers, who included Russian grand dukes as well as bankers and other princes and royalty. She made frequent performance tours of Russia, where she was overwhelmed by the welcome she received, declaring that 'the Russians are my favourite people'. She made the acquaintance of Tsar Nicholas I's grandson, Grand Duke Peter Nikolaievich, and enjoyed telling how in St Petersburg she had been carried in nude on a silver tray during a dinner attended by the grandest men in Russian aristocratic circles, and they had all knelt before her beauty. On such tours she was presented with splendid precious stones and diamonds, which were later used by Paul Amelus to create a platinum bolero entirely studded with diamonds, emeralds, rubies and sapphires. Years later, in 1903, Caroline Otero had the bolero taken apart by Cartier to create a diamond *collier de chien* and a necklace in the form of a ribbon of diamonds terminating in diamond bows and tassels which copied the design of a necklace that had belonged to Queen Marie Antoinette of France.

Caroline Otero's rival on stage at the Folies Bergère was Lina Cavalieri [203–5], who came to Paris from Rome. She travelled to Russia in 1897 to perform in the Krestovsky Theatre in St Petersburg: an event reported the

continued on page 202...

continued on page 202...

OPPOSITE: An early 20th-century advertisement with photographs of some of the most famous and most beautiful artistes of the day, including Lina Cavalieri and La Belle Otero.

196

ABOVE: A poster for the Folies Bergère featuring a much bejewelled Caroline Otero, known as 'La Belle Otero'.

OPPOSITE: Caroline Otero on stage in *Les Rivales*, wearing a necklace of large Oriental pearls.

OVERLEAF, LEFT: Caroline Otero, photographed displaying a great array of jewelry given to her by her many admirers. A large diamond and ruby *devant de corsage* stands out, and from her diamond *rivière* necklace a splendid floral-style ornament made of diamonds and emeralds is suspended.

OVERLEAF, RIGHT: The diamond and emerald centrepiece of Caroline Otero's *rivière* necklace and her *devant de corsage* set with diamonds and rubies.

next day in the first of many newspaper articles: 'La Cavalieri is very young and graceful, and fully justifies the epithet of "La Belle" given to her by a Parisian newspaper. La Cavalieri sang only Italian pieces, with great animation, joy and passion. . . . Her fresh and delightful voice made a great impression.' The city of St Petersburg responded enthusiastically to her performance, responding especially to her beauty.

Caroline Otero and Lina Cavalieri found themselves performing together in July 1898 at the Aquarium in St Petersburg, as the impresario George Alexandrov exploited the rivalry between them. A month later, when a charity event including Lina Cavalieri was announced, the press took delight in recording that the coquettish actress's dress, created especially for the occasion, had cost 40,000 roubles, as it was set with diamonds and precious stones. In the meantime, she had made the acquaintance of Prince Alexander Bariatinsky, and when she left Russia she took with her some fabulous rubies which he had given her as a present. She returned to Russia in the autumn as the guest of the Prince, who introduced her to St Petersburg high society. There were rumours, never confirmed, that the two were married. 'Sasha', as Lina Cavalieri called the Prince, was always ready to humour her every whim, and lavished fabulous jewelry on her.

With her lifestyle so profoundly changed, Lina decided to become an opera singer. As an artist, she was already a model of the ideal woman – beautiful, refined, and regal in her movements. Prince Bariatinsky paid for singing lessons in St Petersburg with Maddalena Mariani-Masi, a distinguished singer for whom the composer Amilcare Ponchielli had written *La Gioconda*. Her operatic debut, in Lisbon, was not a success, and her relationship with Prince Bariatinsky was doomed to failure, as the rigid protocol of the Russian court could not accommodate an artist from the theatre (Bariatinsky went on to marry Princess Yurievsky). The most beautiful jewelry in Lina Cavalieri's collection came from her time in Russia. She subsequently became a respected singer, and at her performances, whether in *Fedora* or *La Traviata* or *Tosca*, she sparkled on stage, not just because of her voice but also because of her splendid jewelry.

Paris was also the scene of a cultural revolution in jewelry design. René Lalique was the undisputed master of this new form, producing pieces with luxuriously soft lines inspired by nature, as feminine forms merged into butterflies. His chosen materials were entirely different from

Opposite: Cover of an issue of the magazine *Femina* for 15 April 1909, celebrating the return of the 'famous singer' Lina Cavalieri from a 'triumphant tour' of America and announcing her forthcoming appearances at the Paris Opéra. She was often shown displaying the strings of pearls seen here.

Année. N° 198.

Le Numéro : 50 cent.
Le 1ᵉʳ et le 15 de chaque mois.

Femina

Mlle LINA CAVALIERI

La grande cantatrice, après une triomphale saison en
Amérique, vient de rentrer en France et a signé un engagement avec l'Opéra de Paris, pour y donner une brillante
série de représentations dans les grands rôles du répertoire.

(Reutlinger.

Opposite: Lina Cavalieri in a photograph which shows why she was so famed for her beauty. Around her neck the soprano is wearing a necklace of three strands of pearls encircled by brilliant-cut diamonds. Pearls were her favourite jewels.

Above: Grand Duke Alexei, uncle of Tsar Nicholas II, photographed with Lina Cavalieri while attending the Grand Prix in Paris. It is said that the Grand Duke was more used to the sound of champagne corks popping than cannon fire.

Opposite and above: Head ornaments designed by Georges Fouquet, including splendid examples of bandeaus in aquamarine *plique-à-jour* enamel and diamonds, with spaces for aigrette plumes of feathers.

those of the stiffly formal garland style, which looked back to the style of Louis XVI and used the most expensive stones [208–9]. Lalique and his contemporaries such as Georges Fouquet [206–7] used much less valuable materials, such as horn, glass, and especially enamel, and they chose stones more for their chromatic effects than for their intrinsic value. Among Lalique's most regular clients was Sarah Bernhardt, the greatest actress of the Belle Epoque.

If Caroline Otero and Lina Cavalieri came from Paris to Russia, an artistic movement in reverse occurred when Paris was spellbound by Sergei Pavlovich Diaghilev's Ballets Russes, founded in 1909 [210–13]. Diaghilev's infallible musical intuition led him to discover the young composer Igor Stravinsky, after having heard him perform in a private concert at the St Petersburg Conservatoire. Thus began a fruitful relationship that was cemented by a mutual appreciation of the two men's artistic talents. The Paris public was swept away by the hectic atmosphere of the revolutionary Ballets Russes' performances of Stravinsky's *Firebird*, *Petrushka*, and *Rite of Spring*. Diaghilev found a protector in Paris in the Comtesse Greffulhe, famed for her elegance and for her great artistic sensibilities, who was also president of the Societé Musicale Indépendante, an organization founded by the publisher Gabriel Astruc to promote new music. (Her role in Paris was similar to the one played for the Ballets Russes in London by the Marchioness of Ripon.) The stars of Diaghilev's company were the dancers Vaslav Nijinsky [211] and Tamara Karsavina; Anna Pavlova was engaged for particular performances. Nijinsky's talent was such that whereas ballets had previously been written to show off the skill of ballerinas, they now began to be conceived for male dancers (examples are *Le Spectre de la Rose*, *Petrushka*, *Narcisse* and *Le Dieu Bleu*).

The last performance of the 1909 season was *Cléopatre*, superbly performed by Ida Rubinstein in fabulous costumes by Leon Bakst [212]. Bakst played a crucial role in the presentation of the Ballets Russes, his memorable backdrops and costumes with their rich vivid colours evoking the spirit and sensuality of Russia. The writer Jean Cocteau was struck by

continued on page 214...

ABOVE: An outstanding example of the garland style is this necklace created in 1894 by Chaumet in Paris, with its design of bows and sprigs of flowers echoing the Louis XVI style realized in diamonds and oval and cushion-cut sapphires.

OPPOSITE: An exceptional group of jewelry created by René Lalique between 1898 and 1904. These are splendid examples of the new Art Nouveau style, of which Lalique was the undisputed master.

"SHEHERASADE"

JANE MARNAC

BAKST

OPPOSITE: A preparatory sketch by Leon Bakst for a costume for the ballet *Scheherazade*.

RIGHT: A poster for the ballet *Le Spectre de la Rose*, with a painting of Vaslav Nijinsky by Jean Cocteau.

BELOW: Jean Cocteau and Diaghilev.

LA SAISON RUSSE A PARIS : CLÉOPATRE

Parmi les attractions de cette saison russe qui a été le véritable événement de la saison parisienne a figuré le ballet de Cléopâtre, où Mlle Ida Rubinstein mima le rôle de Cléopâtre, avec une grâce de gestes et une étrangeté d'attitude qui enthousiasmèrent l'assistance charmée. (Voir page 351, les Danseuses russes au Châtelet).

ABOVE: Ida Rubinstein in the role of Cleopatra, costumed by Leon Bakst, in 1909.

OPPOSITE, INSET: Cover of *Femina* magazine featuring Caterina Gheltzer, 'the star of the Russian season in Paris'.

OPPOSITE: Vera Fokina and her husband Michael Fokine in the ballet *Scheherazade*.

Mᵉ GHELTZER, LA DANSEUSE ÉTOILE DE LA SAISON RUSSE A PARIS

the ballet *Scheherazade*, based on a symphonic poem by Rimsky-Korsakov. In *Scheherazade* Bakst recreated the Arabian Nights through colour combinations never before seen, such as emerald green and intense red with electric blue: Cocteau commented that the performance had 'splashed all Paris with colours'. The critic André Varnod wrote that 'all fashion is now taken up with the Ballets Russes, as no house can be without green and orange cushions, and women have started to dress in garish colours.'

In response to this excitement, the couturier Paul Poiret liberated women from their corsets by creating clothes with soft lines and Oriental detailing, and launched a fashion for turbans adorned with large feathers

ABOVE: Head ornament with movable pendants in briolette-cut and antique-cut diamonds, surmounted by a large aigrette plume of feathers.

OPPOSITE AND OVERLEAF: Guests at the Comtesse Aynard de Chabrillan's 'Mille et une Nuits' Ball, held in 1912. The costume worn by the Infante Ferdinand of Spain (top left) was originally designed by Bakst for the ballet *Le Dieu Bleu*.

Infant Fernand d'Espagne.

M^{ise} d'Argenson.

Ctesse B. de Clérmont-Tonnerre.

P^{cesse} Guy de

Mme Goloubew.

M. André de Fauquières.

Mme H. de Sinçay.

Cte H. de Fe

Ctesse A. de Chabrillan.

M^{ise} de Lévis-Mirepoix.

Mlle de Caillavet.

Bénardaky.

Mme Hart.

B^{onne} A. de Neuflize.

M. Francis de Croisset.

Pommereau.

or aigrettes. In 1912 many jewellers started to make aigrettes with plumes of exotic feathers held in place with precious stones. Paris was the setting for fabulous Orientalizing balls. The 'Mille et une Nuits' or 'Thousand and One Nights' Ball held by the Comtesse Aynard de Chabrillan was particularly memorable [214–17]: it was attended by the grandest members of the French aristocracy, and many of the guests wore costumes designed by Bakst. Paul Poiret then organized the 'Mille et Deuxième Nuits' Ball, and it was generally thought that even the most beautiful Russian ballet could not have equalled it for artistry and magnificence. Another important society event was the Oriental ball held by the Comtesse Blanche de Clermont-Tonnerre, for which the courtyard of her mansion was transformed into a Persian palace, and guests displayed splendid turbans, feathers and richly coloured clothes.

At the start of the 20th century St Petersburg emulated Paris as the setting for memorable society events, which culminated in 1914 in a series of extraordinary balls. At the beginning of the year, Countess Elizabeth ('Betsy') Shuvalov held the 'Ball of the Coloured Wigs' in her palace on the Fontanka Embankment [219]. Equally lavish and exotic was a costume ball held by Countess Kleinmichel: there, Meriel Buchanan, the British Ambassador's daughter, noted in her memoirs, the oriental quadrille was led by the Grand Duchess Cyril – Victoria Melita – and the costumes were designed by Bakst. It was such a success that the dance was repeated on the following evening in the palace of Grand Duchess Maria Pavlovna.

This period of frivolity was destined to end with the assassination of Archduke Franz Ferdinand of Austria and his wife in Sarajevo on 28 June 1914, and the outbreak of the First World War.

OPPOSITE: The Ball of the Coloured Wigs, held in the palace of Countess Elizabeth Shuvalov at the beginning of 1914, was one of the last society events of that particularly dazzling season. In the years before the Great War, high society in St Petersburg could rival that of Paris.

～5～

THE DOWNFALL OF THE TSAR

In 1915, the situation of the Russian army had become seriously compromised by terrible losses of soldiers, uncertainty about the outcome of the conflict, continuous anti-tsarist demonstrations, and growing social discontent. On 5 September Nicholas II took a decision that was to prove fatal for the survival of the tsarist regime: he assumed supreme command of the army and left St Petersburg. The government and the entire imperial family vainly attempted to dissuade him, but the Emperor refused to change his mind and persisted with this dangerous course of action. The Allied governments were deeply disturbed by the news, but were powerless to intervene in the politics of another state. They still wanted Grand Duke Nicholas Nikolaievich to remain at the head of the Russian army. The official reason for his removal was the constant losses suffered; but many felt that the decision stemmed from the Empress Alexandra's jealousy of his growing prestige in military and civilian circles, which was in danger of eclipsing that of the Tsar.

The monk Rasputin was among those hostile to Grand Duke Nicholas, ever since at the start of the conflict he had telegraphed the Grand Duke to ask for permission to bless the troops departing for the front, and the Grand Duke had responded: 'If you come, I'll hang you.' Rasputin's sinister influence on the imperial couple was one reason for their increasing unpopularity. A native of Petronovskoye, a small village near the city of Tobolsk in Siberia, Grigory Yefimovich Novykh was known as 'Rasputin' or 'Dissolute'. After an ill-spent youth, he felt the call to religious life and went on pilgrimage first to Damascus and then to Jerusalem, after which he quickly gained the reputation of being a holy man (*starets*) or a healer with the gift of prophecy. He arrived in St Petersburg in 1905, and his fame as a healer soon spread rapidly through the city, especially through the salons of high society. His circle of admirers even included public

OPPOSITE: The daughters of Nicholas II, photographed in 1914. In the main picture they are, from left to right, Grand Duchesses Maria, Tatiana, Anastasia and Olga; inset are further images of Tatiana and Olga.

figures and members of the imperial family, such as the sisters Anastasia and Militza, wives of Grand Duke Nicholas Nikolaievich and his brother Peter. The two Grand Duchesses were nicknamed 'Scylla' and 'Charybdis' by the family because of their interest in the occult, and it was through them that the Empress Alexandra made Rasputin's acquaintance in 1907, when she was particularly distressed by the Tsarevich Alexei's haemophilia.

All consultations with the greatest medical authorities and the most respected healers of the time had proved ineffective, and the child's suffering was increasing. Rasputin demonstrated that he could stop little Alexei's haemorrhages simply with the power of prayer. With this unexpected improvement in the Tsarevich's health, the Empress became ever more influenced by Rasputin, who soon became her confidant and adviser. This provoked bitterness and hostility on the part of her enemies, and she had to defend herself against vicious rumours about her reputation and her relationship with the monk. She refused to listen to warnings from the Romanov family, or from important members of the government. The latter presented her with many documents from the Okhrana (the secret police) proving Rasputin's corruption and thus the impropriety of the Empress continuing a relationship that was disgracing her public image, but she was deaf to every warning.

The situation reached crisis point when the Tsar left for the front in September 1915. Sir George Buchanan, the British Ambassador to St Petersburg from 1910 to 1918, wrote in his memoirs about a meeting with the Empress early in September 1915:

> During an audience with the Empress I told Her Majesty that I shared the fears of the Council of Ministers regarding the Emperor's decision, as not only would His Majesty have to assume the entire responsibility for whatever new disaster might befall his army, he would also have to combine the duties of the commander-in-chief with those of an autocrat of a vast empire and this task was thought to be beyond the strength of any single man. The Empress objected at once saying that the Emperor should have taken command at the very start and now that his army was showing signs of a deep crisis, his place could only be at the side of his troops. She then went on to say: 'I have no patience with the ministers who are trying o prevent him from doing his duty. The situation requires firmness. The Emperor, unfortunately, is weak; but I am not and I intend to remain strong.' Her Majesty did not change her view. While

OPPOSITE: Nicholas II and Alexandra with their children, *c.* 1914. The Grand Duchesses are, from left to right, Maria, Tatiana, Olga and Anastasia.

BELOW: Nicholas II in the summer of 1913 at Peterhof, with his two older daughters dressed as honorary regimental colonels. Olga (on the left) is wearing the uniform of the Hussars and Tatiana the uniform of the Uhlans. This parade was the last time Mathilde Kschessinska saw the Tsar: in her memoirs she recorded with great emotion how proud the Emperor was on this occasion when he was accompanied by his daughters.

OPPOSITE: Tsarina Alexandra and the Tsarevich at an official ceremony.

the Emperor was at the front he was unable to stay in constant contact with his ministers, and was too absorbed in military problems to be able to take care of internal political issues arising from the increasingly serious situation; and so the Empress was effectively governing Russia, particularly after Stürmer became President of the Council in February 1917.

The continual changing of ministers (on Rasputin's advice) increased the discontent felt towards the government and the imperial family. In the resulting political upheaval many people, including several members of the Romanov family, felt that Rasputin was the dark heart of this tragic situation.

On the insistence of the Dowager Empress and her daughters, Xenia and Olga, Grand Duke Nicholas wrote to the Tsar to inform him of Alexandra's ever greater interference in the affairs of state. Despite the advice of several members of the family, the Tsarina was unshakable, and would not discuss Rasputin, even when her sister Elizabeth warned her: 'Remember the fate of Louis XVI and Marie Antoinette.' Events reached such a point that a plot involving Grand Duke Dmitri (the son of Grand Duke Paul) and Prince Felix Yusupov was hatched to kill the monk. They were successful, and on 19 December 1916 Rasputin's body floated to the surface of the icy waters of the River Neva. The two men were sent into exile, but the Empress was deprived of Rasputin's support.

The country was now becoming unstable, with daily unrest in the factories and more than two hundred thousand striking workers swelling the ranks of anti-war marchers; slogans hostile to the tsarist government appeared ever more frequently on the streets of Petrograd, and the scarcity of food and lack of fuel to heat people's homes added to the chaos. In late February 1917 many army regiments united with the revolutionaries, criminals were released from prisons, and policemen were gunned down in exchanges of fire in the streets. Nicholas II still did not realize how dangerous the situation had become: he refused to appoint a minister responsible to the Duma and decided to return to the capital.

An interim committee had been formed in Petrograd under the leadership of Mikhail Rodzianko, and he and the Duma took power. Nicholas II's train was stopped by revolutionaries and diverted to Pskov, where the Tsar was forced to sign the abdication document in favour of Tsarevich Alexei. However, he feared that separating his son from the rest of the family might affect the Tsarevich's health, so a few hours later he abdicated instead in favour of his brother, Grand Duke Michael Alexandrovich.

On 22 March 1917, Nicholas II joined the rest of his family – the Tsarina, Tsarevich, and the Grand Duchesses – at Tsarskoe Selo, and their internment began in the Alexander Palace. This confinement was not meant to last very long. There was a proposal to move the family to England, but this kept being postponed, as the interim government attempted to calculate the political effects of such a decision, and no-one was prepared to commit himself for fear of being compromised.

In June that year the activity of the Bolsheviks began to be very strong both in Petrograd and in the provinces. Count Benckendorff, Grand Marshal of the Court, in his memoirs wrote about this period:

> Lenin, Zinoviev, Trotski and all the fanatics who have up to this moment governed our unfortunate country by terror, and have landed it in shame and opprobrium, had already appeared on the scene, and their party gained ground from day to day in the Soviets of workmen and soldiers, and everybody was astonished at the weakness shown by the Provisional Government towards them.

The situation became extremely dangerous for the imperial family with the increasing successes of the Bolsheviks. Their armed revolt was put down, but Alexander Kerensky did not have the courage to eliminate the leaders. At

THE GREATEST IMPERIAL TRAGEDY:
LAST DAYS OF THE EMPEROR NICHOLAS II. AND HIS FAMILY.

The entourage of the imperial family during their internment at Tsarskoe Selo in the summer of 1917. Countess Benckendorff is in the foreground; behind her are Prince Basil Dolgorukov, Pierre Gillard, Countess Hendrikov, Baroness Buxhoeveden, Miss Schneider, Count Benckendorff and Dr Derevenko.

Grand Duchess Tatiana seated in the park at Tsarskoe Selo, guarded by
two soldiers.

the beginning of July he became President of the Council, but he was not
able to handle the increasingly alarming riots in Petrograd. In the middle of
July he came to Tsarskoe Selo to explain to the Tsar that it would be safer for
him and his family to leave and settle far away in the countryside: he suggested that they start packing at once, and make the preparations as secretly
as possible. The Tsar and Tsarina chose the people they wished to accompany them: Baroness Buxhoeveden, Countess Hendrikov, Miss Schneider,
Prince Basil Dolgorukov, Dr Botkin and Pierre Gillard, the Grand Duchesses'
tutor. At the end of July Colonel Kobylinski, the commandant in charge of
the imperial family, told them that their departure had been arranged for
1 August, without disclosing the destination. The Tsar wrote in his diary:

> Our last day at Tsarskoe Selo. Marvellous weather. . . . After dinner
> waited for the departure hour to be set, which they kept postponing.
> Unexpectedly Kerensky arrived and declared that Misha [the Tsar's
> brother Michael] would arrive soon. Indeed, at about 10:30 dear
> Misha walked in accompanied by Kerensky and the chief of guards.
> It was very nice to see him, but awkward to talk in front of outsiders.

228

Grand Duchess Olga, the Tsarevich, and Grand Duchesses Anastasia and
Tatiana, resting after working in the garden.

At midnight the imperial family, their suite (except for Baroness
Buxhoeveden, who was ill) and their servants were gathered together in
the great salon of the Alexander Palace. The train had been ordered for
1 o'clock in the morning, but it was late, and not until 7.30 were the
family settled in the train, and the destination disclosed as Tobolsk
in Siberia.

Count Benckendorff remained at Tsarkoe Selo, and before leaving he
was able to arrange a meeting with Mr Golovin, the Commissioner for the
Ministry of the Court, who took possession of the palace. In their
conversation he asked him to take the necessary precautions for its safety
and that of the numerous objects of value which the Tsar had left there.
Mr Golovin agreed that the objects of value should be transferred to the
repository of the Imperial Office in the Anichkov Palace. Count Benckendorff
also drew the Commissioner's attention to the jewelry that belonged to the
Tsarina personally, which had been deposited in the store-rooms of the
Imperial Office. He also mentioned that Princess Victoria of Battenberg,
the Tsarina's sister, who was in Russia when the war broke out,
in passing through St Petersburg to return to England via Finland and

ABOVE: The salon in the Alexander Palace at Tsarskoe Selo where the imperial family were gathered together at midnight on 1 August 1917 to be transferred to Tobolsk in Siberia.

OPPOSITE: A cushion-cut diamond with a deep amber yellow colour weighing 102.55 carats mounted as a pendant with a border of diamonds by Bolin. This jewel appeared at an auction in Stockholm in the early 1920s as the property of an 'anonymous vendor'. Newspaper articles at the time reported that it was part of the collection of the imperial Russian crown, but other sources maintained that it had belonged to Tsarina Alexandra, and that she had taken it together with other pieces of jewelry hidden in a cushion to Tobolsk, from where it then disappeared. (The diamond was later known as the Ashberg diamond after its new owner.)

Sweden had given her jewels to her sister for safety. The Tsarina had sent them to the Imperial Office in a sealed case. Mr Golovin made a note of this, but the fate of the jewels is unknown.

Nicholas II, Alexandra, their family, suite and servants arrived at Tobolsk on 6 August 1917; on 13 August they moved into Freedom House (the governor's house), and there they lived fairly comfortably until the end of April 1918.

From Tobolsk the family were taken to Ekaterinburg in the Urals. The Soviets chose the house of the engineer Nikolai Ipatiev, and surrounded it with a high fence so no-one would be able to see inside. In this house, renamed 'the house of special purpose', the imperial family were to spend their last days in privation and humiliation. The Tsar and Tsarina and their eldest daughter, Olga, were brought there first. To her daughters who were still in Tobolsk, the Tsarina wrote that they should bring 'medicines' – their code word for jewelry – to Ekaterinburg. Quite certain that they would soon be rescued by the White Army, she was adamant; so, ignoring the advice of their entourage, the Grand Duchesses took the jewels with them rather than leaving them in the security of Tobolsk. (Some major pieces were, however, entrusted by the Tsarina for safekeeping to the abbess of the convent in Tobolsk.) With the help of their governesses, Sasha Tegkleva and Liza Ersberg, they managed to hide some jewelry by stitching it between two corsets, while loose stones, such as diamonds and pearls, were disguised as buttons or sewn into clothing. It is likely that other pieces were hidden in the cushions that the Grand Duchesses always carried with them.

In the meantime Grand Duke Michael had moved to a hotel in Perm with his English secretary Brian Johnson, his valet, and his driver. On 12 June 1918 in the evening three soldiers arrived at the hotel and abducted the Grand Duke and Johnson: they were taken to a nearby forest, shot in the head, and their bodies hidden under twigs and then buried later in the night.

On 4 July, Commander Avdeiev, the head of the guard responsible for the custody of the imperial family, was replaced by Yakov Yurovsky. He introduced himself to the prisoners, and explained that, because they were under arrest, they would have to hand over their jewelry and that, for reasons of security and in order to prevent any thefts, a record would have to be made of the jewels. Yurovsky and his assistant, Grigory Nikulin, took charge of the jewelry, and Nikulin made an inventory with a description of the pieces. The jewelry was then kept in a sealed box, which was checked every day to ensure that it had not been opened.

Photographs from the archive of Nikolai Alexeievich Sokolov (see
pp. 236, 266) showing two rooms in the Ipatiev house in Ekaterinburg as
they were found after the imperial family had been murdered in the cellars.
The lower photograph shows the bedroom occupied by the Tsar, Tsarina
and Tsarevich.

The house of Nikolai Ipatiev in Ekaterinburg where the imperial family
and their retainers were held prisoner. The Bolsheviks erected the wooden
fence to prevent anyone seeing in.

On 8 July, a special room in the basement of the house was prepared in
expectation of the execution of the prisoners, pending an order from Moscow.
The situation in Ekaterinburg had become particularly tense because the
White Army were approaching. Yurovsky and his soldiers had planned who
among them would fire at the heart of which member of the family, and a
coded telegram was sent to Lenin in Moscow to obtain ultimate approval.

In the middle of the night of 16 July 1918 Yurovsky woke Nicholas II,
his family, and four members of their suite and told them to prepare for an
immediate departure. The prisoners were led into the basement of the

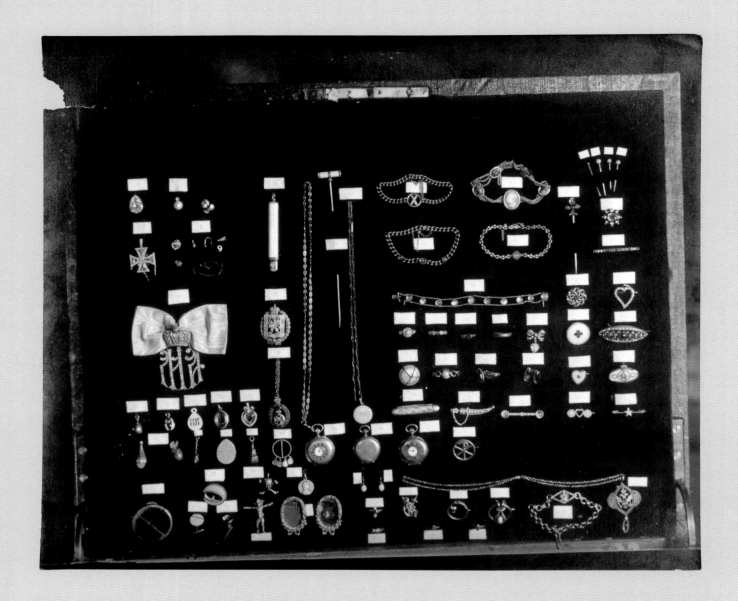

house; the Tsarina asked for chairs for herself and her son Alexei, while the others remained standing. At this point Yurovsky opened the door and called in the waiting firing squad; the sentence of death was quickly read, and they opened fire. The Tsarina just had time to make the sign of the cross before she fell with her husband. The Grand Duchesses, however, did not fall at once because the bullets bounced off the corsets they were wearing, into which the strings of diamonds had been sewn. This caused great consternation among the soldiers, who had to use bayonets to kill them. The bodies were then taken to a nearby wood. As they were being stripped,

ABOVE: A photograph from the Sokolov archive of imperial jewelry left behind at Ekaterinburg by the Bolsheviks and found by the White Army. Much of it had been surrendered by the Tsarina and Grand Duchesses to Yurovsky before their death; some had been discovered.

OPPOSITE: A photograph from the Sokolov archive of jewelry found in the area of the mineshaft where the bodies of the Romanovs were first buried, including one of the Empress's earrings, a pear-shaped diamond and a pendant in the shape of a cross.

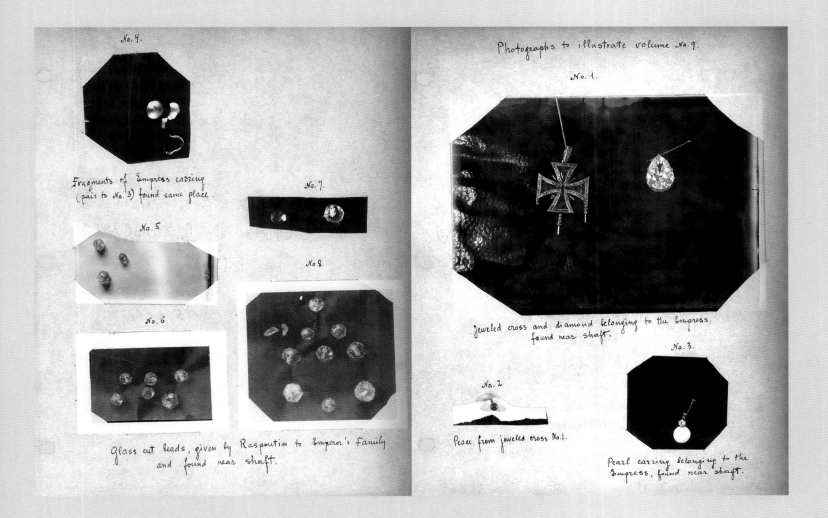

No. 4.

Fragments of Empress earring
(pair to No. 3) found same place.

No. 5

No. 6

No. 7.

No 8.

Glass cut beads, given by Rasputin to Emperor's Family
and found near shaft.

Photographs to illustrate volume No. 9.

No. 1.

Jeweled cross and diamond belonging to the Empress,
found near shaft.

No. 2.

Piece from jeweled cross No.1.

No. 3.

Pearl earring belonging to the
Empress, found near shaft.

the guards noticed that diamonds were falling out of the Grand Duchesses's corsets which had been ripped by bullets, and inside the Tsarina's belt several strings of pearls were found. The soldiers rushed to remove the jewels. The bodies were then hacked into pieces, thrown into an old mineshaft, dissolved in sulphuric acid, and burned, all so that the White Army should not find any trace of the slaughter.

Yurovsky went back to Ekaterinburg with a sack full of the jewels found on the bodies that weighed almost 18 lbs (9 kg), and decided to bury them in the cellar of a house in the neighbouring village of Alapaevsk (where other members of the Romanov family were to be murdered: see p. 236). Not until 1919 were the valuables dug up and taken to Moscow.

In the excitement some of the jewels had fallen to the ground, and these were later found by the White Army (see p. 236), who had been told of the massacre by local people. At the spot to which the bodies had been brought, a drop-cut diamond weighing some 12 carats, probably hidden under the Tsarina's clothes and thus saved from the Bolsheviks, was discovered. After this dramatic end, many legends grew up around the imperial family and their jewelry.

~6~

DISPERSAL AND SURVIVAL

On 25 July 1918 the city of Ekaterinburg had been captured from the Bolsheviks by Siberian and Czech troops, and White Army soldiers found evidence of the Romanovs' stay in the Ipatiev house and of their subsequent disappearance. An investigation began under a member of the court, M. Sergeiev: he failed to complete it, and all the material evidence and personal effects of the imperial family that had been found were handed over to Admiral Kolchak, head of the unified anti-Bolshevik admin-istration. After a few months the inquiry was placed in the hands of Nikolai Alexeievich Sokolov, who was the official investigator for cases of exceptional importance. He began by studying the evidence collected by his predecessors, and meticulously compiled a dossier rich in photographs and documents [234, 235]. Sokolov also discovered the fate of other members of the Romanov dynasty: Grand Duchess Elizabeth, Grand Duke Sergei Mikhailovich, Prince Vladimir Pavlovich Paley and Princes Ivan, Constantine and Igor Constantinovich had all been murdered at Alapaevsk near Ekaterinburg (cf. p. 235) twenty-four hours after the shooting of the Tsar and his family.

A truce was concluded in 1922 after the revolution and ensuing civil war and the new government had to begin the task of reconstructing the devastated national economy. The fabulous treasure of the Romanovs, which included gold, diamonds and the most beautiful precious stones, a symbol of the *ancien régime*, had become the property of the Russian people after the fall of the Tsar. Many rumours circulated about its fate,

OPPOSITE: A photograph from the catalogue compiled under the supervision of A. E. Fersman showing some of the historic diamonds belonging to the Russian Treasury. In the centre is the Orlov diamond, mounted on the imperial sceptre. It is flanked by four views of the Shah diamond [304], with an inscription on each side. At the top are three views of the diamond that decorated the imperial orb [33]. The large diamond bottom right was sold in London in 1927 as lot 100 (see p. 260).

ABOVE: The first photograph of the treasure of the Romanovs appeared on 23 September 1922 in an article in *L'Illustration*.

and it was suggested by some that the Bolshevik leaders had plundered the Treasury. It is certainly true that many pieces had been secretly taken out of Russia, both when the imperial and aristocratic palaces were looted and when the banks were nationalized.

Nine enormous chests filled with priceless objects were removed from the Armoury Chamber in the Kremlin in Moscow and stored in a secure place by the representatives of the people. (Documents discovered in the office of the Armoury Chamber shortly after the Revolution show that much had been taken from the chests between 1914 and 1916.) The treasure of the imperial crown remained in custody in Moscow until 1922, when an initial inspection was carried out by a special committee appointed by the new government with the aim of making an inventory of all that remained of the Tsar's collection.

An article that appeared in the French journal *L'Illustration* on 23 September 1922 was the first to include a photograph of the table upon which the crown jewels were displayed beneath the watchful gaze of the members of the government committee. The article went on to say:

We have received a document of great interest from America: a photograph of the imperial crown jewels of Russia. This is the first photograph that the Soviets have allowed to be taken since this treasure fell into their hands. Some explanatory notes were included. They state that an assessment of the jewels has been carried out in Moscow on behalf of the Soviets by an expert 'French' jeweller, Monsieur Fabergé, and that the total value amounted to sixty billion dollars! . . .

Our own intelligence allows us to add some more definite information. The Soviets' first concern, on the day after the revolution, was to plunder all the jewelry in Russia, whether it belonged to the crown or was private property. The total value of this .'. . expropriation is estimated to be seven billion francs. A committee of 63 members was appointed to ensure the preservation of these riches and to evaluate them with the intention of selling them. But a certain number of people assigned to this task took part in illegal trafficking. All the members of the committee were brought before tribunals and 21 of them were shot, while the others were sentenced to various periods of imprisonment.

A new committee has been appointed. In the photograph, we can see some of its members. . . .

The treasures displayed on the table are the authentic imperial crown jewels; it would appear that no major piece has been removed or, at least, not one which is known to the specialists. . . . The photograph which we publish here was taken recently in Moscow, so the Soviets have not yet dismembered the imperial crown jewels, and the way in which the first committee entrusted with their safekeeping was treated is an indication that they do not intend to allow any clandestine trafficking of this treasure which they have reserved for their own commercial benefit.

Professor A. E. Fersman, a leading figure in the Russian Academy of Sciences, had been appointed as the head of the committee, and given the task of registering and describing the contents of the imperial chests; he was assisted by experts on *objets d'art* and jewelry. The committee had to carry out its work without being able to refer to any previous complete inventory. Every single piece was photographed, and all stones were weighed and their particular characteristics described. Some documents came to light which helped the committee to discover who had made the jewelry.

Since the 18th century, the chests containing the jewels had been kept in the Diamond Room, as the strong room in the Winter Palace in St Petersburg was known. Officially called the 'Regalia and Crown Jewels' or the 'Diamonds and Pearls of His Imperial Majesty's Private Estate', the treasure was entrusted to the care of appointed keepers in His Imperial Majesty's Wardrobe Service, which was part of His Imperial Majesty's Cabinet. According to various documents, nothing from the crown jewels could be removed from the Diamond Room without prior written consent.

Two diamond and ruby brooches of bow design, dating from the end of the 18th century.

Once this had been obtained, the piece of jewelry could only be taken away in the presence of a trustee, appointed by the Emperor. At the outbreak of war, the Imperial Council had decided to move the treasure to Moscow, where it was under the supervision of Monsieur de Bentichev, a trustee of His Imperial Majesty's Wardrobe Service. The chests were moved in such a hurry that there was no time to compile a list of contents when they left St Petersburg. They arrived at the offices of the General Headquarters and were subsequently moved to the Armoury Chamber. Those were the nine chests subsequently found after the fall of the Romanovs.

The jewels now to be inventoried also included pieces recovered from the Dowager Empress Maria Feodorovna's private apartments in the Anichkov Palace, where she had had them transferred for her own

A *devant de corsage* and girandole earrings of diamonds and spinels by Leopold Pfisterer, signed and dated 10 April and 27 May 1764.

use. An inventory of her holdings made in 1909 recorded seventy-seven items, but when they were found by the Bolsheviks the number was considerably reduced. It is highly likely that between 1909 and the beginning of the Revolution some precious pieces had been taken back to the Armoury Chamber.

Among the jewels found in the apartments of the Dowager Empress was a large bow-shaped *devant de corsage* with pendant. This fabulous piece is inscribed on the reverse with the name of Leopold Pfisterer, the jeweller who designed it, and the date of its completion – 'Pfisterer, 10 April 1764' – together with the weight of the stones. It is set with 21 spinels with a total weight of 150 carats; the backs of the stones are covered with foil to accentuate their colour, in a typical 18th-century closed mounting of solid gold. The brooch forms part of a *parure* with girandole earrings: these are signed and the weight of the stones is again given; their date is 27 May 1764. Here too the spinels are enclosed in a solid gold mounting and backed with foil to accentuate their colour.

The crown jewels include a wonderful set of sapphires and diamonds which are an exceptional example of gems from the time of the Empress Elizabeth, *c.* 1750 [*opposite*]. An aigrette suggesting a fountain decorated with diamond jets of water from which hang briolette-cut sapphires is said in an accompanying document to have been the personal property of the Empress. It formed part of a *parure* with a pair of pendant earrings designed as a cascade of diamonds and sapphires, also with diamond jets of water, from which hang briolette-cut sapphires.

Among the pieces the committee decided to save was a group of extraordinary diamond jewelry from the Empress Elizabeth's time [*overleaf*]. A bodice ornament designed as a bouquet of flowers is described in Fersman's catalogue:

continued on page 248...

OPPOSITE: An aigrette and girandole earrings in diamonds and sapphires suggesting cascades that belonged to the Empress Elizabeth, *c.* 1750.

OVERLEAF: A magnificent group of jewels from the end of the time of the Empress Elizabeth, *c.* 1760. All the diamonds are of Indian and Brazilian origin, and all are mounted in solid gold and silver with a foil to accentuate their hues. From left to right, they are: an extraordinary *devant de corsage* in the form of a bouquet of flowers, set with diamonds and Colombian emeralds; a smaller bouquet, with leaves in gold and dark green enamel; a pair of earrings designed as roses with a bee on the flower and green enamel leaves; and a bouquet of narcissus, the pistils in diamonds of yellow tint, the petals of colourless diamonds and the leaves in green enamel.

PRECEDING PAGES, LEFT: A diamond girdle with two tassels made in the reign of Catherine the Great, attributed to Louis David Duval. Part of it was used to create the nuptial crown seen opposite.

PRECEDING PAGES, RIGHT: Diamond epaulettes. The first two date from the beginning of the 19th century; the third is a gold epaulette from the time of Catherine the Great.

LEFT: Princess Elizabeth of Saxe-Altenburg on the day of her wedding in 1884 to Grand Duke Constantine Constantinovich. (She became Grand Duchess Elizabeth Mavrikievna.) She is wearing the nuptial crown and the jewels worn by all Romanov brides.

OPPOSITE: The Russian nuptial crown, created *c.* 1840 from elements of the great 18th-century diamond girdle (preceding pages, left).

This 'bouquet' [244] was called by a French connoisseur 'le plus merveilleux bijou du dix-huitième siècle', and indeed one may truly say it has but few rivals in our Collection or elsewhere.

The perfect incidence of white and green, the originality of design, so light and graceful, are combined here with exquisite workmanship. Thin gold stems and leaves, liberally sprinkled with emeralds, set off shapely gemmed flowers, the whole forming a fragrant many-hued nosegay.

Each part attached on plume-like supports, the bouquet swings freely, throwing forth countless fires at the slightest touch.

This 'bouquet' was worn as a bodice ornament. Although some details of the general scheme remind one of the Elizabethan style (1760), this work is nevertheless characteristic of Duval's manner.

The diamonds in this unique piece are fine Golconda and Brazilian stones of different hues, from violet to pink and yellow, set in solid gold.

The imperial nuptial crown [248, 249] was created in 1840 by the jewellers Nickol and Plincke using diamonds set in the great girdle of the time of Catherine the Great, attributed to the famous 18th-century jeweller Louis David Duval. The surviving part of the girdle, with two diamond tassels [246], is composed of separate parts joined together with silver wire; the stones are mounted in solid silver. In the crown the diamond trimmings are sewn onto crimson velvet and fastened on the surface with silver threads.

The nuptial crown was used by all the Russian grand duchesses and wives of grand dukes on their wedding day, together with the diamond tiara of the Empress Elizabeth Alexeievna [50, 51], the *collier d'esclave* [53] and the diamond earrings and great diamond clasp of the time of Catherine the Great. Nevertheless, it was not considered a very artistic object, and was included as lot 62 in the 1927 sale of imperial jewels in London (see below). What remained of the girdle, on the other hand, was regarded as a noble example of mid-18th-century jewelry and retained by the Russian government.

continued on page 256...

OPPOSITE AND ABOVE: Jewels worn by Russian grand duchesses and wives of grand dukes on the day of their wedding, together with the *collier d'esclave* and the nuptial crown [53, 249]. They are the great clasp of Catherine the Great's imperial mantle, attributed to the court jeweller Jérémie Pauzié; diamond earrings in the form of cherries; and a tiara decorated with Indian briolette diamonds, with at its centre the Paul I pink diamond, weighing 13 carats. (Foil behind this diamond that intensified its colour was recently removed.)

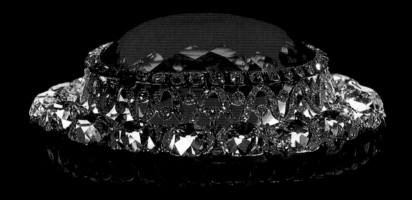

OPPOSITE: Two views of an oval multi-faceted sapphire found in the Dowager Empress Maria Feodorovna's private apartments in the Anichkov Palace; it weighs 260 carats and is set in a typical Russian mounting encircled by 18 diamonds weighing approximately 50 carats.

ABOVE: The Sinople Queen emerald weighing more than 136 carats, in a mounting of diamonds of the time of Nicholas I.

OVERLEAF: Members of the first unofficial Fact Finding Commission to Russia inspect the crown jewels of the Romanovs, shown to them in Moscow by permission of the Soviet authorities in November 1926.

The Romanovs were famous for their collections of emeralds, which were certainly among the finest stones in the Imperial Treasury. They include a square step-cut emerald known as the Sinople Queen [253], of an intense deep green colour, weighing more than 136 carats. It is thought that this stone was found in South America in the middle of the 16th century; in the time of Nicholas I it was mounted in a border of old-cut diamonds in silver settings alternating with leaves decorated with diamonds. It was deposited in the Cabinet of His Imperial Majesty in 1913 along with the collection of the recently deceased Grand Duchess Alexandra Iosifovna (née Princess of Saxe-Altenburg), consort of Grand Duke Constantine Nikolaievich and mother of Queen Olga of Greece.

Two notable sapphires featured among the jewels. Alexandra Iosifovna's collection included a splendid antique sapphire from Ceylon (now Sri Lanka), cabochon in an almost circular shape, weighing 197 carats; in the mid-19th century it was set in a typical Russian mounting edged with tiny circular diamonds and surrounded by a border of large antique-cut diamonds. Perhaps the most beautiful sapphire is one that was found in the Dowager Empress Maria Feodorovna's apartments – a stone weighing 260 carats, also set with diamonds in a typical Russian mounting [252].

In order to raise funds, in 1926–27 the Bolshevik government came to the decision to sell some of the jewelry from the Crown Treasury. A commission was set up to select what was to be sold, and 124 lots were chosen, some of which included several pieces, such as the floral diamond ornaments of the time of Catherine the Great. Pieces of greatest importance to the history of Russia, and those from the great 18th century, were retained, including the coronation regalia and the historic diamonds. Fortunately the government did not destroy that splendid page in the history of jewelry-making in Russia and the world.

Regrettably, however, they did destroy the jewels of the time of the last Tsar, considering them to be modern and not of historic importance. The diamond crown made by Hahn in 1896 for the coronation of the

Two of the imperial jewels sold at Christie's in London in 1927.

OPPOSITE, ABOVE: The diamond and drop pearl *kokoshnik* (lot 117), made by the court jeweller Bolin in 1841, came from the apartments of the Dowager Empress Maria Feodorovna.

OPPOSITE, BELOW: The bracelet is one of two diamond bracelets from the reign of Catherine the Great, *c.* 1780, designed with bands of foliage and ribbon, with a knot of ribbon in the centre around a large oval diamond (lot 44).

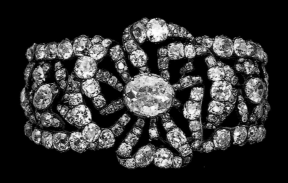

Left and below: Girandole earrings in amethysts and diamonds, from the second half of the 18th century, which were sold in 1927 (lot 27). They reappeared on the market recently.

Right: Diamond tassels from the period of Catherine the Great, designed by Duval, sold in 1927 in sixteen lots, each comprising two tassels. They reappeared recently at an auction mounted as earrings.

Below: The crown jewels and the committee assigned to select the pieces to be sold at Christie's in London in 1927.

Opposite: An article that appeared in the *Sphere* magazine a few days after the sale.

THE ROYAL REGALIA OF THE ROMANOFFS.

The First Reproductions in Colour of the Russian State Jewels, Acquired by an English Syndicate, and Sold a Few Days Ago at Christie's Auction Rooms

The Nuptial Crown: A Crown Entirely Composed of Double Rows of Fine Brilliants in Borders of Smaller Stones, and Surmounted by a Cross of Six Large Brilliants, the Whole on a Setting of Red Velvet

A Magnificent Brooch, with Diamond Foliage-pattern Groundwork, the Top Set with a Superb Emerald, an Oblong Spinel and Two Sapphires in the Centre, and Three Large Pear-shaped Pearl Drops

A Green Jasper Snuff-box Set with Multi-coloured Diamonds of the Period of Louis Quinze

A Diamond Tiara Added to the Regalia After the Death of Marie Fedorovna

A new significance was given to the phrase "Scratch a Russian and you find a Tartar" recently, for the sale of a portion of the Russian State jewels brought to London a display of almost Oriental brilliance. Crowds thronged the sale-rooms in St. James's Square of Messrs. Christie, Manson and Woods, both before and during the auction, to view the glittering array. The first reproductions in colour of four of the pièces de resistance are shown above. The nuptial crown—one mass of blazing diamonds—which was used at the weddings of the Imperial House, was perhaps the most remarkable exhibit, but the workmanship in the diamond tiara, wrought in the form of wheat-ears and set with a large white sapphire, is so delicate that the entire coronal trembles at the slightest touch.

An accurate valuation of the collection, brought together mainly during the eighteenth century, when Russia emerged as a European entity of the first class under the sovereignty of Peter the Great and Catherine the Great, is impossible of achievement. The auction realised a stupendous sum which, nevertheless, must be regarded as its minimum price, for trade buyers formed the major portion of the purchasers. Perhaps the most romantic exhibit in the whole collection was the Tsar's sword, the hilt of which is a coruscant mass of brilliants, although a green jasper snuff-box of Louis Quinze design, set with diamonds of varying hues, rivalled its multi-coloured fire. The sum realised constitutes a record, for the greatest previous total produced by a sale of jewellery was £150,000

ABOVE AND OPPOSITE: The wall cavity in the Yusupov Palace in Moscow where the treasure belonging to the family was found, and two views of the palace.

Empress Alexandra was dismantled and the stones sold separately. The same fate befell the diamond *rivières* with their big cushion-cut stones, mostly of Indian or Brazilian origin, which were much easier to sell unmounted and separately than in a large single piece of jewelry.

The sale of the imperial jewels took place in London at Christie's, on 16 March 1927. The title-page of the catalogue read: 'An important assemblage of Magnificent Jewellery Mostly dating from the 18th Century which formed part of the Russian State Jewels And which have been purchased by a Syndicate in this Country. They are now Sold in order to close the Partnership Account'. A magnificent oval brilliant-cut diamond of pinkish tint, of approximately 40 carats, mounted as a brooch [237] (lot 100), and a *kokoshnik* set with twenty-five large pearl drops in old-cut diamond borders [257] (lot 117) were among the jewels found in the apartments of the Dowager Empress Maria Feodorovna in the Anichkov Palace. Also in the sale was the nuptial crown [249] (lot 62), and among the 18th-century jewels a pair of magnificent diamond earrings of girandole design (lot 45) and many floral ornaments in diamonds.

Two years earlier, in 1925, the treasures of the Yusupov family had been discovered by chance. They had been hidden, as we have seen (p. 159), in a niche in the family's palace in Moscow. After the Revolution, the building had become the Museum of Military History. The head keeper became curious about some cracks which had appeared in a wall, and informed the director of the museum. To his great surprise, this particular wall proved to be relatively new. He ordered it to be demolished in order to see what might be hidden behind it, and discovered the

priceless cache. The collection immediately became state property, and a team of experts carried out a detailed inspection.

In the photograph taken at the time, showing the group of specialists involved in assessing the jewelry [*overleaf*], it is possible to recognize the complete *parure* of emeralds and diamonds designed by Chaumet in 1914 which was a wedding present from Prince Felix to his wife, Princess Irina. Also visible is the delicate rock crystal and diamond tiara made by Cartier, which had been presented by Princess Zenaida to her daughter-in-law, who would have worn it on her wedding day to hold her veil in place. In the foreground is the pearl and diamond tiara worn by several

continued on page 266...

OVERLEAF: The treasure of the Yusupov family and other Romanov jewels being examined by experts – and, in the case of some pieces, broken up – prior to its valuation and sale.

261

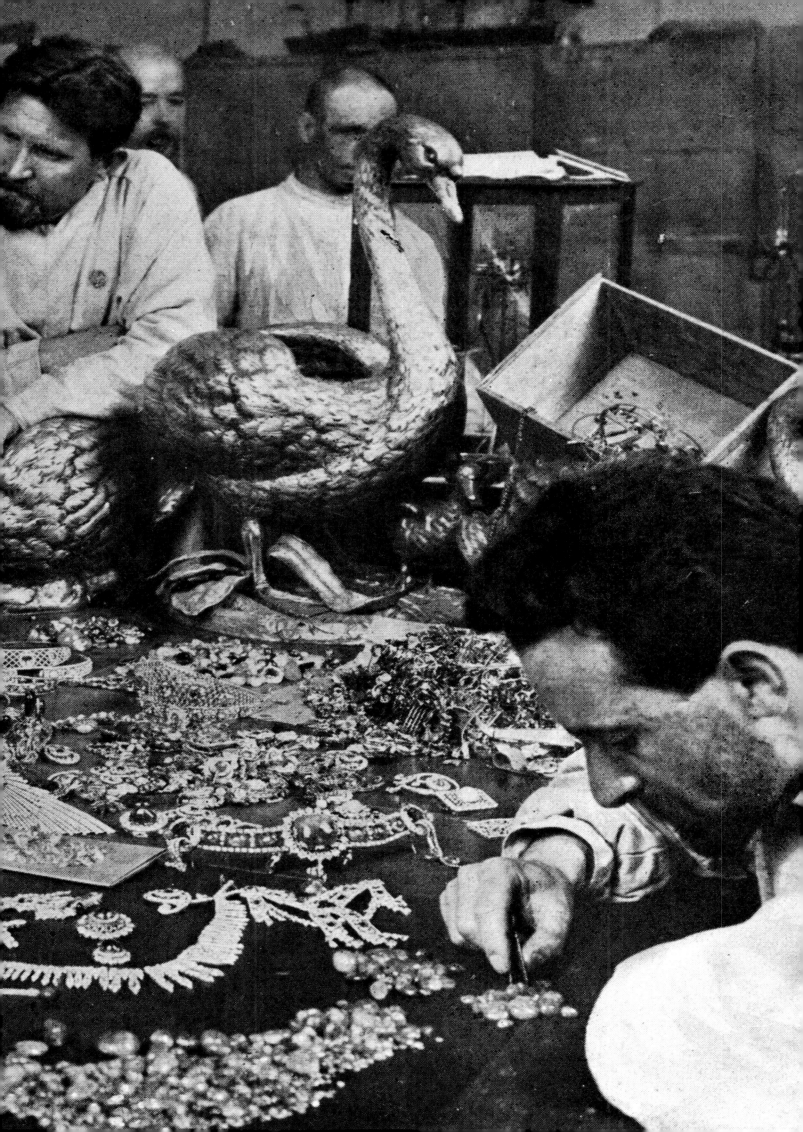

BELOW AND OPPOSITE: Designs for *parures* for Grand Duchess Xenia:
in diamonds and emeralds (below: see p. 62), in rubies and diamonds
(opposite, above: see p. 63), and all diamonds (opposite, below: see 64).
All were destroyed along with the Yusupov treasure. Some appear already
broken up in the photograph of the jewels being examined [*preceding pages*].

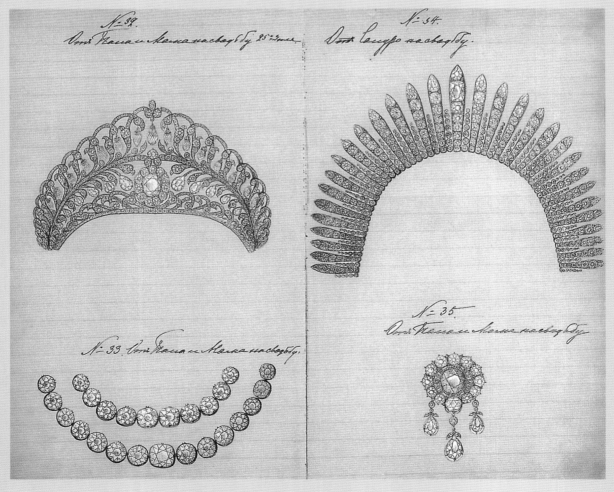

princesses of the Yusupov family. The most striking pieces of jewelry in the photograph, however, are those belonging to the Grand Duchess Xenia Alexandrovna, Princess Irina's mother, which were entrusted to Prince Felix to hide along with the treasures belonging to his own family. The photograph also shows in its form as a necklace the *tiare russe* which was a wedding gift from Grand Duke Alexander Mikhailovich to Grand Duchess Xenia.

Jewelry which Tsar Alexander III and Tsarina Maria Feodorovna gave to their daughter for her wedding can also be seen, including a diamond and cabochon emerald tiara; a diamond tiara decorated with briolette-cut diamonds; and the ruby and diamond sections which formed a tiara and matching ruby and diamond necklace. On the left, it is possible to recognize the diamond brooch with three pear-shaped diamonds in the hand of one of the expert evaluators. Unfortunately, the photograph was obviously taken because the experts intended to remove the stones from their settings. On the right of the picture, is a pile of settings which are ready to be melted down and stones are apparently arranged in lots, most probably in order to be sold on the international market. This marks the destruction of some of the most beautiful examples of the work of French and Russian goldsmiths.

The Dowager Empress Maria Feodorovna had escaped in April 1919 to England, where her sister Alexandra was the Queen Mother, and eventually early in 1920 settled in her native Denmark in Hvidøre, a villa on the coast that the two sisters had bought in 1906 after the death of their father, King Christian IX [268]. Nikolai Alexeievich Sokolov would have liked to present the dossier he had prepared to her, but she declined to receive him and refused to examine the dossier, though she did contribute a large sum of money to continue the investigation. She could not accept that her son and his family were dead, and for the rest of her life she believed that they were safe. In Denmark she divided her time between Hvidøre and the Amalienborg Palace in Copenhagen. On Good Friday 1920 Maria Feodorovna was joined by her daughter Olga and Olga's husband Nikolai Kulikovsky and their two sons, Tikhon and Gury. Later that year Olga was very happy to have her maid, Mimka, arrive at the villa. It had taken her two years to walk from St Petersburg, but she had managed to save some of the Grand Duchess's jewelry by sewing it in the hem of her skirt, including a diamond bow brooch from the time of Catherine the Great.

OPPOSITE: Sapphire and diamond brooch with pearl pendant, bought by Queen Mary of Great Britain in 1929 from the personal collection of the Dowager Empress Maria Feodorovna.

The year 1923 saw the last gathering of the surviving members of the Romanov dynasty on the occasion of the wedding of Prince Feodor Alexandrovich, son of Grand Duchess Xenia, and Princess Irina Pavlovna Paley, daughter of Grand Duke Paul [271]. A month earlier, Xenia and her mother, Maria Feodorovna, had attended the wedding of the Duke of York – the future George VI – and Elizabeth Bowes-Lyon.

On 13 October 1928 Maria Feodorovna died at Hvidøre. During her exile she had jealously guarded the box of jewelry that she had brought with her from Russia, and she left both jewelry and house to Xenia and Olga. The house was sold, and Olga used her share of the money to buy a farm in Denmark, where she lived for many years with her family. To avoid difficulties over the jewelry, Xenia and Olga's cousin George V sent Peter Bark to Denmark to collect the casket and transfer it to safety in London.

Bark insured the contents of the jewel box for £200,000 and took it to the British Legation in Copenhagen, whence it was transported by

A diamond bracelet decorated with a sapphire, a pearl and a ruby,
purchased by King George V of Great Britain from the Empress Alexandra's
private collection.

The Dowager Empress Maria Feodorovna and her sister, the British Queen
Mother Alexandra, photographed in their residence at Hvidøre in Denmark.
Maria Feodorovna has pinned on her dress the diamond brooch of the Order
of St Andrew.

A diamond and pearl brooch which belonged to the Dowager Empress Maria Feodorovna and was sold by Grand Duchess Xenia to Lydia, Lady Deterding.

train to London. It was opened in Windsor Castle in the presence of George V and Queen Mary, Grand Duchess Xenia and Sir Frederick Ponsonby; the 76 pieces in it were examined, Xenia selected the jewelry that she wanted to keep for herself and her sister, and the rest was entrusted to the London jewellers Hennell's of Bond Street for a valuation which took place in Windsor Castle on 29 May 1929. Queen Mary, who was especially fond of jewelry, took the opportunity to acquire the finest pieces from Maria Feodorovna's collection, including a pearl *collier de chien* with a diamond clasp and a central cabochon sapphire, and the diamond brooch with a cabochon sapphire and a drop pearl that had been given by the Prince and Princess of Wales to Dagmar when she married Grand Duke Alexander – the future Tsar Alexander III – in 1866 [267].

The most important piece in the whole treasure was a necklace of thirty-two large pearls. King George bought it for his wife for £64,000, and it seems likely that this is the necklace that Queen Mary left to her son Edward, which was later worn by his wife, the Duchess of Windsor. George V also bought a bracelet composed of a string of decorated diamonds with a sapphire, pearl and ruby centrepiece, and gave it to Queen Mary as a Christmas present that year.

Grand Duchess Xenia, who had retained her magnificent pearls, sold them in a series of unfortunate transactions, which ended in a lawsuit in 1933 because the sum agreed was never paid to her. On the advice of Sir Frederick Ponsonby, Keeper of the Privy Purse, George V assisted the Grand Duchess by appointing Peter Bark as her financial adviser and paying her a pension of £2,400 a year. He also gave her Frogmore House in the grounds of Windsor Castle as a grace and favour home. Xenia later sold a brooch composed of a large pearl encircled by diamonds, from which hung another circular pearl which supported a final drop pearl [*above*], to Lydia, Lady Deterding, the wife of the Dutch petrol magnate. Maria Feodorovna appears wearing this brooch in a portrait and in photographs that show her holding the infant Tsarevich, the future Tsar Nicholas II, in her arms.

Just as the daughters of the last Empress sold their jewelry, so too did the other members of the Romanov family. Grand Duchess Maria Pavlovna died at Contrexéville in France, where she had chosen to retire, in 1920. Her jewelry had been kept by Cartier in Paris, where it was catalogued and valued. After the pieces had been photographed, they were divided between the Grand Duchess's four children. Grand Duke Cyril, who escaped from Russia with his wife Victoria Melita and their daughters, managing to bring his wife's jewelry, received the sapphires. The beautiful sapphire and diamond *kokoshnik* created by Cartier in 1909 was sold by his wife to her sister, Queen Marie of Romania. Boris received the emeralds, which he sold back to Cartier [100–101]. Andrei received the rubies, including the diamond and ruby *kokoshnik*, also designed by Cartier, with the Beauharnais ruby set in the centre. This piece was purchased by Nancy Leeds in 1921, when her son William Bateman Leeds married Princess Xenia Georgievna of Russia, daughter of Grand Duke George Mikhailovich and Princess Marie of Greece – a close friend of Grand Duchess Xenia, who was the young Princess's godmother. Elena received the diamonds and pearls, and sold the tiara with the intertwined arches of diamonds with pendant pear-shaped pearls to Queen Mary of Great Britain.

On 15 October 1922 the coronation of King Ferdinand and Queen Marie of Romania was celebrated in the city of Alba Iulia, in the recovered region of Transylvania. Marie had lost all of her jewelry, as she sent it to Russia at the outbreak of the First World War where she believed it would be safer, but it was stolen during the Revolution and no trace of it was ever found. She wrote in her memoirs: 'Both my jewels and legal tender of the country to the amount of 7 million gold francs were sent by the National Bank of Romania, together with many artistic treasures, to Moscow and were never returned.' She decided to recreate her collection, and so in 1921 she commissioned Cartier to create a pearl and diamond tiara. That same year, King Ferdinand purchased – with the proviso that the sale could be annulled if any serious or unforeseen events

OPPOSITE: The wedding of Irina Pavlovna, Princess Paley (daughter of Grand Duke Paul and Olga, Princess Paley), and Prince Feodor Alexandrovich in the Russian Cathedral of St Alexander Nevsky in Paris on 31 May 1923. Standing behind the bride, from left to right, are Grand Duke Dmitri Pavlovich (her half-brother), Grand Duchess Xenia (the bridegroom's mother), the bridegroom, Grand Duke Alexander Mikhailovich (the bridegroom's father), Princess Paley (the bride's mother), and Grand Duchess Maria Pavlovna the Younger (her half-sister).

271

intervened and that the payment could be made in four instalments by 1924 – a long diamond *sautoir* from which hung the largest sapphire in the world, which had a pear-shaped cut and weighed 478 carats, for his wife to wear on the day of their coronation [*opposite*]; the *sautoir*, created in 1911, had been bought back by Cartier from Nancy Leeds.

A crown was also created for her by the French jeweller Falize in Byzantine taste, of gold set with turquoises and amethysts.

ABOVE: Queen Marie of Romania at the reception for her coronation in Alba Iulia on 15 October 1922. She had removed the Falize crown and put on her diamond and sapphire *kokoshnik* (made by Cartier in 1909 for Grand Duchess Vladimir [p. 114], inherited by her son Grand Duke Cyril, and sold by his wife Victoria Melita to her sister Marie) to complement the diamond *sautoir* from which hung the great sapphire, seen opposite.

OPPOSITE: A photograph from the Cartier archive of the diamond *sautoir* from which hung a 478-carat sapphire, bought in 1921 by King Ferdinand of Romania for Queen Marie, which she wore at her coronation. The sapphire recently reappeared in an auction at Christie's in Geneva.

ABOVE: Queen Marie of Serbia – 'Mignon' – and her sister, Queen Elizabeth of Greece, dressed for the coronation of their parents, King Ferdinand and Queen Marie of Romania, in 1922. Marie is wearing Grand Duchess Elizabeth's emerald and diamond *kokoshnik* and necklace [277–79] with at its centre the brooch. King Alexander I of Serbia had bought the jewels from Grand Duchess Maria Pavlovna the Younger as a gift for his bride in 1922. Elizabeth is wearing her mother's pearl and diamond tiara created by Cartier in 1921.

OPPOSITE: A photograph from the Cartier archive of the *sautoir* created by Cartier for Queen Marie of Serbia in 1923 using the emeralds and diamonds from the necklace and brooch of Grand Duchess Elizabeth which she had worn in their original form in 1922.

Of the coronation, Queen Marie wrote: 'I emerged in my red-golden underdress, a crimson velvet mantle lined with silver-blue on my shoulders, and on my head a golden veil bound round my forehead with a golden ribbon over which the crown was to be placed, my "grand cordon" and star! . . . my two queenly daughters were a joy to the eye, each in her own way [275]. Lisabetha was in a sort of golden moiré, which looked like a lizard-skin, with a mantle of the same tissue. On her head was a golden veil and a diadem of pearls and diamonds . . . Mignon was also in gold with an orange-velvet mantle which she had ordered especially as it is my favourite colour . . . on her head was a golden veil and her superb emerald and diamond diadem which Sandro [King Alexander] had given her for her wedding.'

The year 1922 saw not only the coronation of the King and Queen of Romania but also the wedding of their daughter, Princess Marie (called 'Mignon' by her family), to King Alexander of Serbia (later Alexander I of Yugoslavia). For the wedding, King Alexander bought the fabulous emeralds that the Russian Grand Duchess Maria Pavlovna the Younger had received from her aunt, Grand Duchess Elizabeth [*opposite*]. (Maria Pavlovna had in the meantime divorced Prince Wilhelm of Sweden and had married Prince Serge Putiatin.) The new Queen of Serbia preserved the diamond and emerald *kokoshnik* created by Bolin unaltered [278, 279], but she had the emerald necklace redesigned by Cartier in 1923 [274]. The emeralds were kept in their Russian-style mounting with the double row of diamonds, and this created a spectacular *sautoir*, the termination of which was formed by a chain of diamond links [279] that could be detached and fixed onto a large double-headed eagle brooch also designed by Cartier [287]. The Queen received the *sautoir* when her first son, Peter, was born.

The Romanian Princess Marthe Lucile Bibesco had her famous emeralds [180, 181] remounted by Cartier early in the 1920s in the geometric style of the period [288–91]. The five large cabochon emeralds were set on a specially created diamond tiara in the shape of a *kokoshnik*, which could also be worn as a necklace. There was a brooch, from which hung another large circular cabochon emerald within a diamond motif.

continued on page 284...

Opposite: Grand Duchess Elizabeth wearing the emeralds of her emerald and diamond *kokoshnik* [278] sewn onto a cloth *kokoshnik*, and her emerald and diamond necklace. She later gave these jewels to Grand Duchess Maria Pavlovna the Younger, and they were bought from her by King Alexander of Serbia for his wife.

Elisabeth Grande Duchesse de Russie

ABOVE: A diamond and emerald *kokoshnik* made by the court jeweller Bolin for Grand Duchess Elizabeth [277], given by her to Grand Duchess Maria Pavlovna the Younger, who sold it to King Alexander of Serbia.

BELOW: A pair of diamond pendant earrings that belonged to Queen Marie of Serbia. The two circular-cut diamonds weigh over 20 carats each.

OPPOSITE: Queen Marie of Serbia, daughter of King Ferdinand and Queen Marie of Romania, wearing her diamond earrings and Grand Duchess Elizabeth's *kokoshnik* and emerald and diamond brooch. She has the latter on a diamond chain, on which she could also wear her double-headed eagle brooch by Cartier [287]; shortened, it formed the back of her emerald and diamond *sautoir*.

OVERLEAF: A photograph taken in Belgrade on 22 October 1923, on the occasion of the baptism of Prince Peter, the son of King Alexander and Queen Marie of Serbia. In the foreground, from left to right, are the Duke of York, future King George VI of Great Britain (the baby's godfather), the Duchess of York, Queen Elizabeth of Greece (the baby's aunt), and Queen Marie and King Ferdinand of Romania (the baby's grandparents). Queen Marie is wearing a large head ornament in the shape of a *kokoshnik* set with strings of pearls with at its centre a gem-set motif, and her pearl necklaces.

ABOVE: Queen Marie of Romania wearing a diamond and sapphire *kokoshnik* which had belonged to Grand Duchess Vladimir [114].

OPPOSITE: Jewelry belonging to Queen Marie, inherited by her son, Prince Nicholas, and sold at the Jürg Stuker gallery in Bern, Switzerland, in 1964.

The two pear-shaped emeralds that had originally decorated the garland style necklace [*cf.* 180–81] became the pendants for two long diamond earrings, highly fashionable at the time. Princess Bibesco was immortalized wearing these jewels in a photograph taken when her daughter Valentine married Prince Dimitri Ghika in 1925 [288]. Queen Marie of Romania and her daughter Queen Marie of Yugoslavia (formerly Queen Marie of Serbia) all attended the Orthodox wedding ceremony celebrated by the Patriarch of Romania, in which the bride was accompanied to the altar by her mother. The total weight of the emeralds in Princess Bibesco's two striking jewels [289–91] was approximately 314 carats; the largest circular diamond on top of the tiara weighed some 12 carats. In the early 1960s she sold the emeralds to a dealer; they appeared at auction in 1970 at Christie's Geneva, without any note of their provenance.

These years witnessed new social changes and a great displacement of people. Paris was still the City of Light and a magnet for the international community, and it had the largest concentration of Russian exiles, who became the source of many fabulous tales about the Russian *ancien régime*. They told stories in particular about the princely collections of the Russian aristocrats, and the occasional discoveries of jewelry in the palaces of Petrograd only seemed to confirm these rumours. There was a notorious case of a discovery of a collection of fabulous jewelry in a private residence, which had in the meantime become the headquarters of the American Relief Administration.

Such stories were sometimes not far from reality, as in the case of pieces created by Fabergé for Grand Duchess Vladimir and the collection of cufflinks of Grand Duke Vladimir [293–95]. As we have seen (pp. 128–29),

continued on page 289...

OPPOSITE: A group of jewels from the collection of Queen Marie of Romania inherited by her son Nicholas and sold in Switzerland in 1964. The emerald cameo (top, centre) had come from the collection of Princess Vera Lobanov Rostovsky, sold in Lausanne in January 1920.

OVERLEAF: The wedding of Princess Ileana of Romania, daughter of King Ferdinand and Queen Marie, to Archduke Anton of Habsburg, Prince of Tuscany, in July 1931 at Peles Castle in Romania. Seated in the front row, from right to left, are Queen Marie, the bride, Archduchess Blanca (the groom's mother), the bride's siblings – King Carol II of Romania and the former Queen Elizabeth of Greece – and young Crown Prince Michael of Romania. The bridegroom stands behind his bride. Next to him, far right, is the bride's sister, Queen Marie of Yugoslavia (formerly of Serbia), who is wearing a splendid diamond brooch in the shape of a double-headed eagle by Cartier [*inset*], attached to her diamond chain [279].

they had been taken to the Swedish Legation in Petrograd by a loyal friend in 1918. A rupture in diplomatic relations led to the entire legation's departure from Petrograd, and two cushions containing the precious objects [293] were taken to Stockholm, along with all the diplomatic papers. It is quite likely that this operation was conducted in the greatest secrecy and that the speed of these events, and their accompanying chaos, assisted this secrecy. With the death of Grand Duchess Maria Pavlovna in 1920, the departure of this treasure was completely forgotten.

It was only in 1952 that the two cushions were opened in Stockholm and an inventory was made of their contents. They were then resealed, and another fifty-six years passed until, in 2008, they were found again because of the reorganization of the government archives. Maria Pavlovna's heirs were identified and specialists from Sotheby's were contacted. An auction then took place in London on 30 November

continued on page 292...

OPPOSITE: Princess Marthe Bibesco with her daughter on the day of Valentine's wedding to Prince Dimitri Ghika in 1925. Marthe wears the emerald and diamond jewelry that she had had remounted by Cartier.

ABOVE: Princess Bibesco's emerald and diamond tiara, remodelled by Cartier in the early 1920s.

OVERLEAF, LEFT: Princess Bibesco immortalized with her famous emeralds.

OVERLEAF, RIGHT: Princess Bibesco's emerald and diamond tiara displayed as a necklace, and her pendant brooch, as they appeared in the catalogue of the auction at Christie's in Geneva on 23 April 1970.

2009 which created great excitement and was an enormous success. Generously, the heirs decided to donate the profits from the sale to the restoration of the castle in Schwerin where the Grand Duchess was born, to fund her first official biography, and, above all, to ensure the future of the Russian Orthodox chapel commemorating her husband, Grand Duke Vladimir, dedicated to St Vladimir, which Maria Pavlovna had had built at Contrexéville in 1909. The Grand Duchess had become a member of the Orthodox Church in 1908, and is buried in this chapel together with her son Boris.

Every piece of jewelry conceals a history, sometimes a legend, and there is always something intensely engaging about every piece. Jewelry is linked to memory, and if an object cannot evoke the past, then it remains anonymous, no matter how beautiful it may be. The rediscovery of the Grand Duchess Vladimir's collection allows us to step back in time, to the origins of a rich and evocative history, when the Romanov family ruled Russia for more than three hundred years and left behind an image of astonishing elegance and splendour. A spectacular example of which is St Petersburg itself, where the splendid proportions and the sophistication of the palaces are fused with the fascination of popular Russian art and the intensity of its colours. In this enchanting city, when one visits a church or palace one is struck by the powerful contrast of colours – from malachite green to lapis lazuli blue and the many colours of rare marbles – all set off by the white of a city that for long periods of the year is covered in a thick blanket of snow.

Just like the sumptuous palaces and royal residences, jewelry also has an important role in Russian culture; the skill of the goldsmiths remains unequalled for the beauty of their fabulous coloured enamel-work. Grand history is brought a step closer by the sense of wonder which we feel when looking at the precious jewels preserved in the Kremlin, or at a fabulous creation by Fabergé, and this allows the cult of the beautiful to be continually renewed.

OPPOSITE: Cigarette cases designed by Fabergé, with the pillowcase in which they had been hidden [*cf.* 118, 126–27]. They formed part of the treasure of the family of Grand Duke Vladimir that was smuggled to the Swedish Legation in Russia, taken to Stockholm, discovered there in 1952, sealed up again, and finally sold on behalf of the descendants at Sotheby's in London in 2009. The pillowcase bears the inscription: 'Appartient à S.A.I. la Gr. Duchesse Vladimir' – 'Belonging to Her Imperial Highness Grand Duchess Vladimir'.

Some of the collection of cufflinks of Grand Duke Vladimir, rediscovered in 2008 and sold at Sotheby's in London in 2009.

ABOVE: A pair made by Michael Perkhin for Fabergé, 1897. The ground is of translucent enamel over hatched engine-turning, within a rose-cut diamond border; on this are applied the initials KG – the number 23 in old Slavonic, as the cufflinks celebrated the Grand Duke and Grand Duchess's twenty-third wedding anniversary.

BELOW: A pair celebrating their eleventh wedding anniversary, by August Holmström for Fabergé, of gold with a border of sapphires and diamonds, *c.* 1885. The diamond-set old Slavonic numeral 11 is also readable in Cyrillic as M or MP, for Grand Duchess Maria Pavlovna.

RIGHT: A pair of jewelled gold cufflinks by Friedrich Koechli of St Petersburg commemorating the wedding of Grand Duke Sergei and Princess Elizabeth of Hesse, 1884.

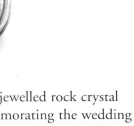

ABOVE LEFT: A pair in jewelled rock crystal and gold commemorating the wedding of George I, King of the Hellenes, and Grand Duchess Olga Constantinovna in 1867, with the initials O in diamonds for Olga and W in rubies for 'Willy'.

ABOVE RIGHT: A gold-mounted rock crystal pair by Samuel Arnd of St Petersburg c. 1880, with Cyrillic VV for Grand Duke Vladimir.

ABOVE: A pair in jewelled rock crystal and gold commemorating the wedding in 1866 of the future Alexander III and Tsarina Maria Feodorovna, with crowned initials – A in cabochon rubies and M in rose-cut diamonds.

ABOVE: A pair celebrating Grand Duke and Grand Duchess Vladimir's tenth wedding anniversary, by August Holmström for Fabergé, 1884. The Cyrillic dates 16 August 1874/1884 are in diamonds, and the Roman numeral X in rubies and sapphires.

RIGHT: A pair celebrating their sixteenth wedding anniversary, by August Hollming for Fabergé, 1890, of rubies and circular and rose-cut diamonds set in gold.

Author's Acknowledgments

My deepest gratitude for helping me with information and photographic material goes to Their Royal Highnesses Prince Michel and Princess Maria Pia de Bourbon Parme; His Royal Highness Prince Dimitri of Yugoslavia; Their Serene Highnesses Princesses Judith and Jean Ghika; Mr Sergey Dmitrievich Shatalov, State Secretary, Deputy Finance Minister of the Russian Federation; Mr Vladimir Borisovich Rybkin, Head of the State Fund of Precious Metals and Precious Stones of the Russian Federation (Gokhran of Russia); Mr Alexander L'vovich Nikolayev, Head of the State Fund of Precious Metals and Precious Stones of the Russian Federation (Gokhran of Russia); Costanza Ciminelli; Penny Gibbard; Luci Gosling; Judith Kolby-Hunt; Simona Oreglia; Diana Scarisbrick; Alexander von Solodkoff; Loredana Stanzani-Ghedini; Dario Tettamanzi; Mark Vivian; and Tess Watts. At Cartier, I am indebted to Bernhard Berger and Betty Jais; at Chaumet, to Mélanie Sallois; at Christie's, to Keith Penton and Raymond Sancroft-Baker; at Sotheby's, to Alexandra M. Rhodes, Irina Kronrod, Darin Bloomquist, David Mountain, Lisa Hubbard and Carol Elkins; and at Van Cleef & Arpels, to Catherine Cariou.

OPPOSITE: A necklace with a bow design, set with diamonds and beautiful Colombian cabochon emeralds; the pyramidal emerald in the centre weighs some 22 carats. Designed by the court jeweller Bolin and made by Sophia Schwan, it forms part of a *parure* commissioned by the Empress Alexandra Feodorovna *c.* 1900 that included a tiara [28] and a *devant de corsage.*

Sources of Illustrations

References are to page numbers

Collection Princess Irina Bagration-Moukhransky 103, 248; Courtesy Cartier Archive, Paris 100, 112 top, 114, 116, 124 right, 272, 274 • Courtesy Chaumet Archive, Paris 111, 153, 154, 155, 157, 158 • Courtesy Christie's 6, 17, 19, 78, 79, 104, 120 above left, 121, 149 centre, 151, 161, 163, 177, 207, 208, 231, 257 below, 258 above, 268, 269, 272 below, 291 • Mary Evans Picture Library 24–25, 29, 37, 47, 54, 56, 58–59, 63, 68, 71, 72, 80, 82–83, 88–89, 92–93, 101 above, 108, 110, 120, 122, 131, 132, 135–38, 143, 152, 168, 176, 178–79, 192, 197, 198, 203–6, 212, 213 above, 215–17, 221, 223–25, 227–30, 238–39, 259, 260, 262–63, 273, 280–82, 286–87 • Getty Images 11, 23, 28, 85, 211 below, 213, 254, 255 • Photo courtesy Hemmelmark Archives, A.v. Solodkoff 113 • Courtesy Mr Ole Villumsen Krog, Registrar of Gold and Silver to H.M. The Queen of Denmark 264–65 • Diana Mandache Collection 273, 275, 279, 286–87 • National Portrait Gallery, London 191 • Private Collection 12–13, 16, 50, 61, 65 below, 90, 95–97, 102, 105, 107, 117, 124 left, 145, 164, 167, 170, 173–75, 180, 181, 184–86, 193–95, 199, 214, 219, 232–35, 270 below, 283, 285, 288–90 • The Royal Collection, Windsor 99 above, 267 • The Smithsonian, Washington, D.C. 149 bottom • Courtesy Sotheby's 2–3, 14, 15, 38, 66, 74, 81, 91, 99 below, 101 below, 109, 112 below, 113 (frame), 115, 118, 119, 126, 127, 139, 140, 141, 149 above left, 162, 182, 188–90, 209, 210, 211 above right, 249, 258 below, 277, 278 below, 287 above left, 293–95 • Courtesy State Fund of Precious Metals and Precious Stones of the Russian Federation (Gokhran of Russia), photographs by Nikolai Rachmanov 1, 31, 33, 35, 39, 47 left, 240–42, 244, 245, 250–53 • State Hermitage Museum, St Petersburg 146 • Photo State Historical Museum, Moscow 48 • State Museum, Pavlovsk 52 • State Museum Preserve 'Tsarskoye Selo', Pushkin 45 • Courtesy Van Cleef & Arpels Archive, Paris 278 top. The following illustrations come from *Russia's Treasure of Diamonds and Precious Stones*, Moscow 1925–26 (catalogue prepared under the supervision of A. E. Fersman) 18, 21, 22, 23 below, 30, 35 right, 40, 41, 44, 46, 49, 51, 53, 57, 60, 75, 106, 165, 237, 246, 247, 257 top.

The aigrette brooch from a *parure* made in 1894 by Chaumet for the Polish Count Lanckoronski, also comprising a tiara, a *devant de corsage* and a necklace [208]. Three cushion-cut sapphires are mounted on a feather motif in diamonds; in the centre is a cabochon sapphire, from which two pear-shaped briolette sapphires encircled by diamonds hang asymmetrically. The garland style saw its greatest expression at the start of the 20th century, when platinum was used to create particularly strong flexible settings with a minimum of metal. This *parure*, although mounted in gold and silver, is still extremely flexible because of the superb workmanship.

Bibliography

Balfour, Ian *Famous Diamonds*, 1987 (5th edn 2009)

Benckendorff, Count Paul *Last Days at Tsarskoe Selo: Being the personal notes and memories of Count Paul Benckendorff, telling of the last sojourn of the Emperor & Empress of Russia at Tsarskoe Selo, from March 1 to August 1, 1917*, 1927

Buchanan, Sir George *My Mission to Russia and other Diplomatic Memories*, 1923

Carbonel, Marie-Hélène, and Javier Figuero *La Belle Otéro sous l'objectif de Reutlinger*, 2009

Catalogue of the Exhibition of Russian Art, exhibition catalogue, London 1935

Clarke, William *Hidden Treasures of the Romanovs: Saving the Royal Jewels*, 2009

Cripps, David William *Royal Cabinet Portraits of the Victorian Era*, 2003

— *Romanovs Revisited, 1860–1960*, 2005

Cyril, His Imperial Highness the Grand Duke *My Life in Russia's Service: Then and Now*, 1939

Desautels, Paul E. *Treasure in the Smithsonian*, 1979

Ferrand, Jacques *Les Princes Youssoupoff et les Comtes Soumarokoff-Elston*,

Fersman, A. E., ed. (The People's Commissariat of Finances / Diamond Fund, Moscow) *Russia's Treasure of Diamonds and Precious Stones*, 1925

Gorewa, Olga W., Irina F. Polynina, Nikolai Rachmanow and Alfons Raimann *Die Schatzkammer der Sowjetunion*, Munich 1990

Habsburg, Geza von *Fabergé / Cartier: Rivalen am Zarenhof*, 2004

— *Imperial Dancer: Mathilde Kschessinska and the Romanovs*, 2005

— and Marina Lopato *Fabergé: Imperial Jeweller*, 1993

Hall, Coryne *Little Mother of Russia*, 1999

— and John Van der Kiste *Once a Grand Duchess: Xenia sister of Nicholas II*, 200

Hatto, Richard J. *Crowning Glory*, 2009

Imperial and Royal Presents, sale catalogue, Sotheby's, London, 24 November 2008

Kejserinde Dagmar, Empress of Russia, exhibition catalogue, Christiansborg Palace, Copenhagen, 1997

King, Greg *The Last Empress: The Life and Times of Alexandra Feodorovna, Tsarina of Russia*, London 1995

Kiste, John van der *The Romanovs, 1818–1959*, 1998

— *Princess Victoria Melita: Grand Duchess Cyril of Russia, 1876–1936*, 2003

Kune, G. F., and C. H. Stevenson *The Book of the Pearl*, 1908

Kurth, Peter *Tsar: The Lost World of Nicholas and Alexandra*, 1995

Mandache, Diana *Later Chapters of my Life: The Lost Memoir of Queen Marie of Romania*, 2004

— *Marie of Romania: Images of a Queen*, 2007

Marie, Queen of Romania *The Story of my Life*, 1935–36

Massie, Robert K. *The Romanovs: The Final Chapter*, 1995

Maylunas, Andrei, and Sergei Mironenko *A Lifelong Passion: Nicholas and Alexandra: Their Own Story*, 1996

Melville, Joy *Diaghilev and Friends*, 2003

Mossolov, A. A. *At the Court of the last Tsar: Being the memoirs of A. A. Mossolov, Head of the Court Chancellery, 1900–1916*, 1935

Nadelhoffer, Hans *Cartier*, 1984 (new edn 2007)

Olga Alexandrovna, Grand Duchess of Russia *25 Chapters of my Life: The Memoirs of Grand Duchess Olga Alexandrovna*, ed. Paul Kulikovsky, Karen Roth-Nicholls and Sue Woolmans, 2009

Ometev, Boris, and John Stuart *St Petersburg: Portrait of an Imperial City*, 1990

Pakula, Hannah *The Last Romantic: A Biography of Queen Marie of Roumania*, 1984

Paley, Princess *Memories of Russia 1816–1919*, 1924

Papi, Stefano, and Alexandra Rhodes *Famous Jewelry Collectors*, 1999

Phenix, Patricia *Olga Romanov: Russia's last Grand Duchess*, 1999

Purcell, Katherine *Falize: A Dynasty of Jewelers*, 1999

Radzinsky, Edvard *The Last Tsar: The Life and Death of Nicholas II*, 1992

Rappaport, Helen *Ekaterinburg: The Last Days of the Romanovs*, 2008

Romanov Heirlooms: The Lost Inheritance of Grand Duchess Maria Pavlovna, sale catalogue, Sotheby's, London, 30 November 2009

The Romanovs: Documents and Photographs relating to the Russian Imperial House, sale catalogue, Sotheby's, London, 5 April 1990

Romanovsky-Krassinsky, H. S. H. The Princess *Dancing in Petersburg: The Memoirs of Kschessinska*, 1960

The Russian State Jewels, sale catalogue, Christie's, London, 16 March 1927

Scarisbrick, Diana *Chaumet: Master Jewelers since 1780*, 1995

Snowman, A. Kenneth, ed. *The Master Jewelers*, 1990

Solodkoff, Alexander von *Russian Gold and Silver*, 1981

— with A. Kenneth Snowman et al. *Masterpieces from the House of Fabergé*, 1984

Sutherland, Christine *Enchantress: Marthe Bibesco and her World*, 1996

Tizio, Franco Di *Lina Cavalieri: La Donna più bella del Mondo: La Vita (1875–1944)*, 2004

Vever, Henri *La Bijouterie française au XIXᵉ Siècle*, Paris 1908

Warwick, Christopher *Ella: Princess, Saint and Martyr*, 2006

Zeepvat, Charlotte *The Camera and the Tsars: A Romanov Family Album*, 2004

A survivor from the Imperial Treasury [237]: the yellow-tinged Shah diamond, weighing some 89 carats, probably from the Golconda mines in India. It bears three inscriptions in Persian: for Burhan Nizam Shah of Ahmadnagar (1591), the Mughal Emperor Shah Jahan (1641), and the Persian ruler Fath Ali Shah (1826), who gave it to Tsar Nicholas I in 1829 after the murder of the Russian writer and diplomat Alexander Griboyedov in Tehran.